do you speak american?

do you speak american?

a companion to the PBS television series

ROBERT MacNEIL AND WILLIAM CRAN

NAN A. TALESE

Doubleday

NEW YORK ★ LONDON ★ TORONTO
SYDNEY ★ AUCKLAND

PUBLISHED BY NAN A. TALESE
AN IMPRINT OF DOUBLEDAY
a division of Random House, Inc.

DOUBLEDAY is a registered trademark of Random House, Inc.

The authors are grateful to the following for permission to quote
the material noted: Cody James, for excerpts from the lyrics of
his song "I'm inspired"; Pronasty Music, for the lyrics of a song
by the Athletic Mic League; Gail Zappa and Munchkin Music
Company for lines from the song "Valley Girl" by Frank Zappa.

ISBN 0-7394-5673-3

PRINTED IN THE UNITED STATES OF AMERICA

CONTENTS

★

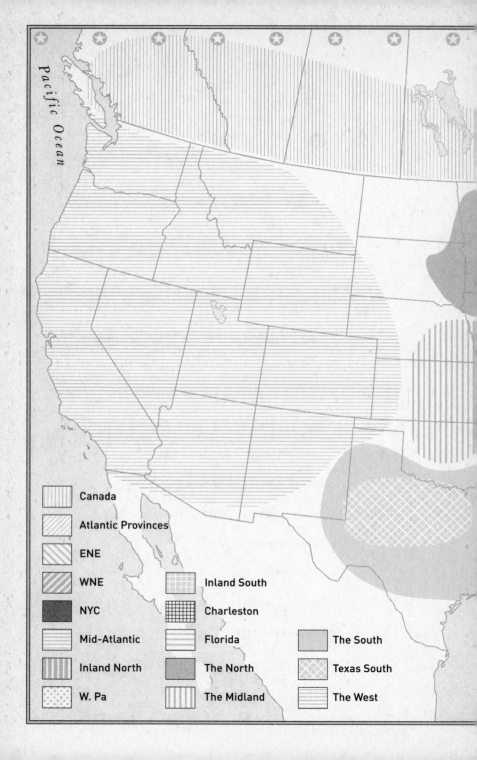

Pacific Ocean

Canada
Atlantic Provinces
ENE
WNE
NYC
Mid-Atlantic
Inland North
W. Pa

Inland South
Charleston
Florida
The North
The Midland

The South
Texas South
The West

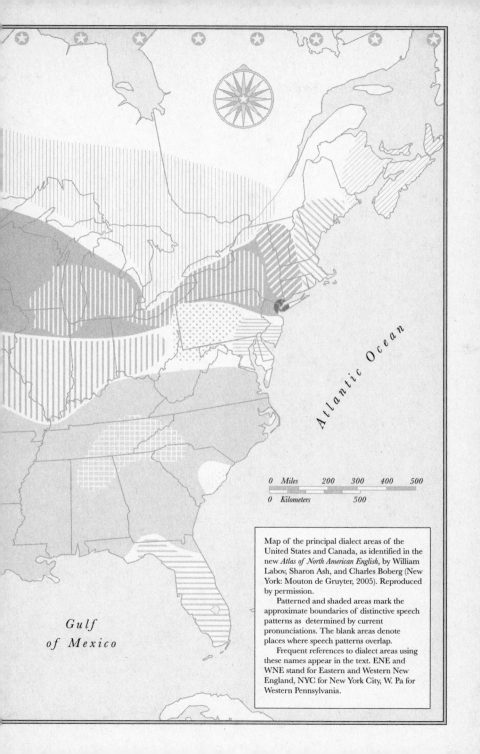

Atlantic Ocean

Gulf
of Mexico

| 0 | Miles | 200 | 300 | 400 | 500 |
| 0 | Kilometers | | 500 | | |

Map of the principal dialect areas of the
United States and Canada, as identified in the
new *Atlas of North American English*, by William
Labov, Sharon Ash, and Charles Boberg (New
York: Mouton de Gruyter, 2005). Reproduced
by permission.

Patterned and shaded areas mark the
approximate boundaries of distinctive speech
patterns as determined by current
pronunciations. The blank areas denote
places where speech patterns overlap.

Frequent references to dialect areas using
these names appear in the text. ENE and
WNE stand for Eastern and Western New
England, NYC for New York City, W. Pa for
Western Pennsylvania.

INTRODUCTION

Our language is constantly changing. Like the Mississippi, it keeps forging new channels and abandoning old ones, picking up debris, depositing unwanted silt, and frequently bursting its banks. In every generation there are people who deplore changes in the language and many who wish to stop its flow. But if our language stopped changing it would mean that American society had ceased to be dynamic, innovative, pulsing with life—that the great river had frozen up. It would be like Latin, a "dead" language that does not change because it lives only in books and few living people speak it. America unceasingly reinvents itself, and it must create language to express that reinvention—in our social mores, in science and technology, in religion, in politics, in the arts—and also to reflect our power and influence in the world.

Curiously and remarkably, John Adams, the future president, foresaw the role of American English even before he knew that the American Revolution would succeed. In 1780, he wrote:

> English is destined to be in the next and succeeding centuries more generally the language of the world than Latin was in the last or French in the present age. The reason of this is obvious,

because the increasing population in America, and their universal connection and correspondence with all nations, will, aided by the influence of England in the world, whether great or small, force their language into general use.

"Whether great or small": it is fascinating that he already imagined such a question in his time.

George Bernard Shaw could joke that "England and America are two countries divided by the same language." But H. L. Mencken argued that American and British speech had evolved so differently that by the beginning of the twentieth century Americans had as reasonable a claim as the British to consider English *their* language.

Voluminously and wittily, and animated by more than a little Anglophobia, Mencken demonstrated that our language began to diverge from the mother tongue almost as soon as the first colonists arrived in North America. He also showed that, for all the British fulminations about American usage, they could not resist adopting Americanisms: "Even *to belittle*, which had provoked an almost hysterical outburst from the *European Magazine and London Review* when Thomas Jefferson ventured to use it in 1787, was so generally accepted by 1862 that Anthony Trollope admitted it to his chaste vocabulary." Recently it was pointed out that the color *robin's-egg blue*, widely accepted in Britain, is an Americanism, because English robins lay brown eggs.

By his fourth edition, in 1936, Mencken had concluded that "the pull of American has become so powerful that it has begun to drag English with it." He even predicted that, with the Englishman yielding so much to American example, "what he speaks promises to become, on some not too remote tomorrow, a kind of dialect of American." Has that tomorrow arrived? We won't be impertinent enough actually to ask the English, "Do you speak American?" The British public would laugh at the notion. Still, British scholars have long conceded that American English is the more influential version of our now global language.

At a news conference in London a few years ago, Prince Charles uttered another of those testy cultural pronunciamentos so endearing to his future subjects. His target was American English, which, he said, tended to "invent all sorts of new nouns and verbs and makes words that shouldn't be." He went on: "We must act now, to ensure that English—and that to my way of thinking means *English* English—maintains its position as the world language." Linguists would challenge Prince Charles on two grounds:

First, the concept of "words that shouldn't be" is alien to the freedom inherent in English. Some people may not like some words, but no one has the authority to forbid their use.

Americans do invent all sorts of nouns and verbs and make verbs out of nouns—as do the British. Some new American verbs may be thought ugly, like *prioritize;* some too close to the cultural edge, like *go commando,* from the TV series *Friends,* meaning to go out without underpants; some too obviously riding the news, like the post-Enron *to be 401k'd;* some extreme *psychobabble,* as in the film *What Women Want,* when Helen Hunt says, "I didn't mean to *guilt* you"; but some just exuberantly creative, as when a flight attendant was overheard saying, "We're late leaving the gate because we *overboarded* the aircraft, so we're going to *comp* the headsets in economy."

It is simply in the nature of English speakers to do this, and of some in every generation to despair. One estimate is that a fifth of all English verbs began life as nouns.

The other response to Prince Charles is that American, not British, English is the engine driving the language globally. Spoken by four times as many people as British, American English reflects America's superpower—or, as the French put it, *hyperpower*—status (love it or hate it) in virtually every field: in literature, fine arts, popular culture, movies, music, television, science, medicine, space exploration, technology, industrial efficiency and productivity, the power of Wall Street, and American military and political might.

As a result, says the *Oxford Guide to World English*, "American English has a global role at the beginning of the 21st century comparable to that of British English at the start of the 20th—but on a scale larger than any previous language or variety of a language in recorded history." The *Oxford English Dictionary* now has to maintain a New York office to keep its database and publications current with American usage.

A *New York Times* story about Americanisms newly adopted by the mother dictionary in Oxford led with this sentence: "Hear the one about the *fashionista* and his *arm candy* who live in *parallel universes*, prefer *chat rooms* and *text messaging* to *snailmail*, suffer *sticker shock* at the cost of *pashminas* and like *chick lit* or *airport novels*?"

Still a revolutionary society in our rapid acceptance of new lifestyles, manners, and morals, the United States, albeit with some backsliding, has been a world leader in recent decades in promoting equality for women and blacks; environmental protection; health, fitness, and dieting; and the reduction of smoking. And our society has undergone a transformation to new levels of informality in clothing, eating, and personal relations.

To communicate all of this, American language adapts. Think, for example, of how *you guys* has now become a generic form of address: it is gender-, age-, and class-neutral, and decidedly informal.

Well, if American English is so vigorous and influential, and millions speak it, why ask, "Do you speak American?" The answer really supposes another question: what *is* American English today, when Americans may speak Cajun, Chicano or Spanglish, Surfer Dude or Valley Girl, the urban black language of hip-hop artists, or any of a dozen other regional or ethnic dialects that together constitute American English—some of them barely intelligible to one another? Add to the mix the extraordinary variety of what is usually considered gram-matically standard American, such as the regional speech differences of broadcasters, or of recent presidents from Massachusetts, Georgia, Arkansas, and Texas. With all that variety, is there even an American English to speak of?

Our question implies still another: Do you consider the American you speak superior or inferior to the speech of your fellow Americans from other regions, social classes, or ethnic groups? Is there a better, or best, American? Most of us have strong opinions on what is good American English and what isn't. Some regional dialects have long en-joyed prestige; others suffer from generations of prejudice. Though some of those prejudices show signs of weakening as American society changes, the backlash of emotional resistance to social change is often expressed in hostility to changing language. As we put it in *The Story of English*, "People tend to fasten their anxieties about the changing world onto words. In the right context, a split infinitive can look like the end of civilization as we know it."

Do You Speak American? is a sequel to *The Story of English*, the BBC/PBS television series on which we collaborated with Robert McCrum in the 1980s.

This is a potent moment in the study of language. In 1940, Aldous Huxley, author of *Brave New World*, complained that for the previous three centuries words had been neglected. A lot of attention had been paid to technical languages of science and mathematics,

> but the colloquial usages of everyday speech, the literary and philosophical dialects in which men do their thinking about the problems of morals, politics, religion, and psychology—these have been strangely neglected. We talk about "mere matters of words" in a tone which implies that we regard words as things beneath the notice of a serious-minded person.

Huxley would have nothing to complain of today except, perhaps, overkill. In the second half of the twentieth century, "mere matters of words" became the study of an ever-expanding branch of the social sciences, linguistics. Not a word, not a piece of a word, escapes attention today.

Linguistics, the science of language, truly flowered as an academic discipline in the 1960s, followed more recently by sociolinguistics, the study of the interaction of language and society. Both have produced a wealth of research, yielding fascinating insights, but these are often technical and not accessible to the general public.

To help us translate their work, many of America's leading linguists have lent their skills to our project. At the end of this book is a list of all the linguists we have consulted, with their affiliations. The TV programs and this book marry these scholars' work to our sampling of the actual speech of ordinary Americans in all their variety, vitality, and humor, drawn from the widest social spectrum. They include waitresses, cowboys, writers and editors, teachers and teenagers, surfers and snowboarders, actors and screenwriters, presidents and state politicians, hip-hop artists, marine drill sergeants, Border Patrol agents and Mexican immigrants, African American and Hispanic broadcasters, Cajun musicians, gay and lesbian activists, and Silicon Valley experts who try to make computers talk like real people.

Our position on that cutting edge in computer development also makes this a timely moment to consider our language. What pressures will come to bear on American English to accommodate technology and the business imperatives behind it? Will there be, for example, an irresistible drive toward a more standardized American, with consequent disenfranchisement, or neglect, of those whose dialects do not conform? That is one of the issues we examine.

The new series, with a major grant from the National Endowment for the Humanities, was filmed throughout the country during 2003. It takes the form of a journey through the most distinctive dialect regions of the United States, from the Northeast through the Middle Atlantic states, to the Great Lakes, down the Ohio River, through Appalachia to the Deep South, then on through Texas and California, ending in the Pacific Northwest.

Linguists draw their own maps to mark different dialect areas. To use the terms in the latest map, "The Linguistic Atlas of North America," we travel through Eastern New England to New York, then to Philadelphia, then west into the Midland dialect, then to the Northern, the Southern, and on to the West.

We address the controversies and issues, anxieties and assumptions, some highly emotional, provoked by language today, and our findings will be news to many.

Whatever effect computers may have in the future, many Americans now believe that our culture's saturation in television and other media is wiping out the differences in our speech, homogenizing the American language, so that we'll all end up sounding the same. Is that true? And how is the language changing, and why?

Why is it, for example, despite decades of advances in civil rights, that white and black Americans are speaking less and less like each other? It is firmly believed by whites (and many middle-class blacks) that street talk or ghetto language is merely bad or lazy English, or that Americans who grow up speaking it are stupid or uneducable. It is also widely believed that if they just made a serious effort black children could easily learn standard American, to pull themselves up by their linguistic bootstraps. We look in detail at these assumptions and what they mean in the long struggle to achieve racial harmony in this country.

Some deeply embedded folk beliefs about language are difficult to dismiss with facts, because people want to believe them.

Some are harmless, like the widespread conviction that Elizabethan, or even Shakespearean, English is still spoken in Appalachia, South Carolina, or Tidewater Virginia—the location varies—but we have a story to put that one to rest.

Other convictions about language today come heavily charged with political intent. Many Americans, hearing more Spanish spoken in their communities, fear that Spanish is becoming a threat to English. They believe that immigration from Mexico and Latin America is of a scale that could linguistically Balkanize the United States. That anxiety is one motive for the movement behind U.S. English, the campaign to make English, by law, the official language of the nation, something it has never been. We examine the facts behind this anxiety: the rate at which Hispanic immigrants are assimilating into mainstream English compared with other immigrant groups in the past; the evidence that Spanish is a threat and the risks some see in playing on this fear.

Finally, many Americans today have a firm conviction that our language is in serious decline, because of falling standards in education, including a neglect of formal instruction in grammar and a more permissive "do your own thing" attitude toward language as toward everything else in the popular culture—dress, eating habits, sexual mores. This trend toward informality has yielded less insistence on rigid codes of conduct during recent decades and a disregard for whatever authorities promulgate them.

Are we Americans ruining the English language? Or as Edwin Newman once put it in a book subtitle, *Will America Be the Death of English?*

one

The Language Wars

> What grammarians say should be has perhaps less
> influence on what shall be than even the more modest
> of them realize; usage evolves itself little disturbed
> by their likes and dislikes.
> —H. W. FOWLER, *Modern English Usage*

For centuries there has been a struggle between those who want our language to obey strict rules and those willing to be guided by how people actually speak and write. The first, who want to *prescribe*, are known as *prescriptivists*, while those content to *describe* usage are called *descriptivists*. The war between the two camps has blazed up with particular belligerence in our times, as language issues engaged social conservatives and liberals and became a factor in the so-called culture wars. Away from that intellectual battleground, ordinary Americans can be either gloriously relaxed about their language or, to use the popular idiom, decidedly *uptight*.

A mild insecurity about language may be part of the American birthright, psychological residue from the one fiber in the colonial cord that was never quite severed. Language uneasiness is rife today, as generations of Americans leave high school much freer socially but without the linguistic confidence of earlier generations, who were better grounded in basic grammar. However informal and tolerant our society becomes, people know that the way they use language still matters. "Aside from a person's physical appearance, the first thing someone will be judged by is how he or she talks," says linguist Dennis Baron.

Fear of such judgment may be feeding the free-floating anxiety that we have found, which manifests itself in adamant doctrines of correctness and the firm conviction that "other people" are ruining the language.

If you cringe when someone says *between you and I;* bristle at the word *hopefully;* detest *prioritize;* if you cherish the distinction between *disinterested* and *uninterested* and deplore their being treated as synonyms; if you wonder what's happened to education when you hear *criteria* used as a singular—then you are probably part of the large body of Americans who feel our language is in a state of serious decline. You may keep it to yourself or feel compelled to express your outrage at every opportunity. But the feelings are strong and very personal. You have the sense of being robbed of something precious to you, to the nation, to our basic cultural values, to your pleasure in knowing you are "correct," to your very sense of identity and where you belong in this society. You believe all of this is being wantonly destroyed by language barbarians among your fellow citizens, who, if you speak up, make you sound out of touch, hopelessly old-fashioned, and quaint in your concerns.

But are you justified in being so upset? Many Americans who also care about the language don't agree with you. For example, Charles Harrington Elster, cohost of the radio program *A Way with Words* on KPBS, San Diego, believes our language "is thriving now probably more than at any time since the Elizabethans." He told the *San Diego Home/Garden Lifestyles* magazine, "I think the language itself is in great shape and growing like Topsy."

Let's begin with those who do think the language is going to hell in this generation. Perhaps the most outspoken is the essayist John Simon. Dapper, cultivated, and acerbic, a leather briefcase tucked under his arm, he is a familiar figure on Broadway as the theater critic for *New York* magazine.

Today, he sees the state of our language as "unhealthy, poor, sad, depressing, and probably fairly hopeless." Hopeless because he sees no improvement in the teaching of English in schools or colleges and "it's been my experience that there is no bottom and that one can always sink lower, or that the language can always disintegrate further."

Simon says all this with a slight lisp and the faintest trace of a foreign accent. But what really gives him away as someone who is not a native-born speaker of English is that his grammar, syntax, and pronunciation are, if anything, almost too polished and correct.

As a child in Yugoslavia, Simon spoke Serbo-Croatian, German, Hungarian, and French, and learned English only in high school. His family moved to the United States at the beginning of World War II, and Simon went on to earn a Harvard Ph.D. in English and comparative literature. He believes that coming to a language late can be an advantage, because one brings better credentials, linguistic, cultural, and emotional.

Simon's own strong emotions about the state of American English came to national attention in 1980 with his book *Paradigms Lost: Reflections on Literacy and Its Decline.* He wrote that language was "better" when he was a graduate student in the 1940s, when "people were not going around saying 'Come to dinner with Bill and I,' or 'hopefully it won't rain tomorrow.' " To explain what started the language "on a downhill course," he offered a sweeping indictment of students, teachers, women, blacks, Hispanics, homosexuals, advertisers, television, and the permissive revolution of the sixties, which dealt education "four great body blows":

(1) the student rebellion of 1968, which, in essence, meant that students themselves became arbiters of what subjects were to be taught, and grammar, by jingo (or Ringo), was not one of them; (2) the notion that in a democratic society language must accommodate itself to the whims, idiosyncrasies, dialects, and sheer ignorance of underprivileged minorities, especially if these happened to be black, Hispanic, and, later on, female or homosexual; (3) the introduction by more and more incompetent English teachers, products of the new system . . . of ever fancier techniques of *not* teaching English, for which, if the methods involved new technologies and were couched in the appropriately impenetrable jargon, grants could readily be obtained; and (4) television—the non-language and aboriginal grammar of commercials, commentators, sports announcers, athletes, assorted celebrities, and just about everyone on that word-mongering and word-mangling medium, that sucks in victims far more perniciously than radio ever did.

In addition, Simon wrote, dictionaries were still relatively "prescriptivist," distinguishing between the correct and incorrect. "Descriptive (or structural) linguistics had not yet arrived—that statistical, populist, sociological approach, whose adherents claimed to be merely recording and describing the language as it was used by anyone and everyone, without imposing elitist judgments on it. Whatever came out of the untutored mouths and unsharpened pencil stubs of the people—sorry, The People—was held legitimate if not sacrosanct by those new lexicon artists."

Simon regarded the publication of *Webster's Third New International Dictionary* in 1961 as a "resounding victory" for descriptive linguistics and "seminally sinister" for its permissiveness. He attacked the "equally descriptive" *Random House Dictionary* and what he called the "amazingly permissive" *Supplements* to the *Oxford English Dictionary*.

Simon was not alone in hating the new *Webster's*. Many did because its editors had dropped the *colloquial* or *slang* labels people were used to. To Kenneth Wilson, a scholar who admired the new dictionary, "nearly everyone who didn't like the book came back to one devastating fault: the book was permissive: it did not tell the reader what was right. It included words and meanings that nice people shouldn't use." He added that "for many it was as though someone had rewritten the King James Version of the Bible or the *Book of Common Prayer* in words taken from the walls of the men's room."

In joining the chorus against *Webster's Third*, John Simon had not just entered the raging "dictionary wars," but had thrown down a most provocative and elitist gauntlet. William Safire, the conservative-libertarian political columnist for the *New York Times*, said Simon made him feel like a "left-winger." In his column "On Language" for the newspaper's Sunday magazine, Safire called Simon "the Prince of Prescriptivists."

In one of the most provocative statements in *Paradigms Lost*, Simon presented an unapologetic defense of elitism:

> Language, I think, belongs to two groups only: gifted individuals everywhere, who use it imaginatively; and the fellowship of men and women, wherever they are, who, without being particularly inventive, nevertheless endeavor to speak and write correctly. Language, however, does not belong to the illiterate or to bodies of people forming tendentious and propagandistic interest groups, determined to use it for what they (usually mistakenly) believe to be their advantage.

The only salvation, Simon concluded, was "the eventual creation of an Academy of the Anglo-American Language." That idea had been around for about three hundred years—and consistently ignored. It was first proposed by Jonathan Swift, on the model of the French Academy, to dictate linguistic standards. His contemporary Daniel Defoe wanted to police the language to the extent that coining a new word would be a crime as grave as counterfeiting money. The English-speaking peoples shrugged that off, as they have all attempts to constrain their language sense. That is why there has been a natural or instinctive rebellion against rules from Latin grammar imposed on English during the seventeenth and eighteenth centuries because certain purists of the day thought our language had grown messy, like an unweeded garden, after the exuberance of Shakespeare and other Elizabethans. Instinctively, unless our high-school English teachers crouch over our shoulders, most Americans naturally say *It's me*, not *It is I*, they split infinitives, many use double negatives, and they end sentences with prepositions.

The Danish scholar Otto Jespersen believed this resistance to arbitrary authority arose from deeply rooted ideas of freedom. Comparing French to the disciplines of a stiff French garden of Louis XIV, and English to the freedom an English park, Jespersen wrote in 1905: "The English language would not have been what it is if the English had not been for centuries great respecters of the liberties of each individual and if everybody had not been free to strike out new paths for himself." If the first shoots of those freedoms sprang up in England, linguistically they flourished even more luxuriantly in America, where they were championed by two great writers of the nineteenth century.

Samuel Clemens (Mark Twain) liberally employed common vernacular language in *Huckleberry Finn* and thus, according to Ernest Hemingway, truly began American literature. Twain argued in 1871: "A nation's language is a very large matter. It is not simply a manner of speech obtaining among the educated handful; the manner obtaining among the vast, uneducated multitude must be considered also." The other champion, Walt Whitman, demanded a real dictionary that "will give us all the words that exist in use, the bad words as well as any."

Many of the slang words are our best; slang words among fighting men, gamblers, thieves, are powerful words. . . . The appetite of the people of These States, in popular speeches and writings, is for unhemmed latitude, coarseness, directness, live epithets, expletives, words of opprobrium, resistance.

There was always this inherent tension in American English: "unhemmed latitude" versus the American schoolmarm. In her literal incarnation she was a strong cultural force as the nation expanded to the west, but a metaphorical schoolmarm was congenial to the American yearning for propriety and gentility, for a homegrown culture that would not be derided by the older cultures of Europe.

Though the free spirit of the new nation produced a torrent of slang and creative English (see the huge dictionaries needed to contain it), what usually found its way into print was strictly *hemmed*. Published American English was expected to mind its grammatical manners; public figures who strayed were corrected by the newspapers that quoted them. So little speech by the common man was recorded that educated Americans could be forgiven the illusion that language, like the wilderness, had been tamed; that the kind of English taught in the schoolroom was America's language.

But under the grammatical veneer was a seething disobedience. Ordinary people, depending on their level of schooling, might make an effort to sound refined when they had to, but free of that obligation just relaxed and used the language as it came naturally to them. They spoke as they dressed: formal suit and tie as infrequently as possible, work clothes or casual duds most of the time.

We know that now because linguists have been able to record their speech, and largely because broadcasting, especially today's television "talk shows" and "talk radio," have flooded the ether with the speech of ordinary people. In one of his commentaries on NPR's *Fresh Air*, Stanford University linguist Geoffrey Nunberg said, "What's different now is that conversation isn't a private affair anymore—it has become the chief vehicle of entertainment and public information. We have become a society of overhearers." And what we overhear is a great range of American English, some of it congenial to English teachers, much not.

After Simon's book became a national best-seller, making him the arch-prescriptivist of the moment, Nunberg published a blistering rebuttal in the *Atlantic Monthly,* chastising "the pop grammarians who play to the galleries." He said there was no hard evidence for a general linguistic decline, adding, "If we are bent on finding a decline in standards, the place to look is not in the language itself but in the way it is talked about." He claimed that Simon's belief in "a morality of language," an obligation to preserve and nurture the niceties, the fine distinctions, that have been handed down to us, "is the credo of a czarist émigré, not an English grammarian."

> Prescriptive grammar has passed out of the realm of criticism, where it sat for two hundred years, to become instead a branch of cultural heraldry. . . . There is nothing in modern writing about the language that is more pathetic than attempts to fix the blame for the "problem" (whatever the problem is understood to be) on this or that small group. If the English grammatical tradition has declined, this is the result of basic changes in our attitude to the language, themselves the consequences of far-reaching social changes. It is not a case of the schools having "failed in their duty."

His article drew one of the greatest volumes of reader response ever. Fourteen years later, in 1997, citing the continuing "fierce interest in language usage," the magazine returned to the fray with "The War That Never Ends," an article by writer Mark Halpern, blasting Nunberg and other descriptivist grammarians, who "suppose that language is an entity with its own laws of development, or natural destiny, and that prescriptivist grammarians are trying to interfere with the course of that natural destiny."

> Nunberg and his allies have no scientific standing in their quarrel with "pop grammarians." . . . They do so not as scientists watching from above the fray . . . but simply as fellow gladiators down in the arena—passionate and opinionated, like their adversaries. How the battle will turn out, how it *should* turn out, no one can say with any authority.

Not only does the war never end, there are few truces. Prescriptivists and descriptivists continue to bombard each other. Of the making of books and articles about linguistics there is no end, and much study apparently does not weary the antagonists' flesh. Some recent books have titles as dire as Simon's. People inclined to be worried about the language will find ammunition, for example, in *The Inarticulate Society.* Author Tom Shachtman argues that American democracy is threatened because we are so dumbing down our language that we risk sliding back to an oral culture, and an "entrenched power structure . . . benefits from a passive and largely inarticulate populace." John McWhorter, a linguist at Stanford, entitled his latest book *Doing Our Own Thing: The Degradation of Language and Music and Why We Should, Like, Care.* He argues that "the sixties swept away lofty oratory and marginalized elaborately constructed prose," to the point where the American public now distrusts formality in language as insincere.

Against such alerts come books with a descriptivist, "stop worrying" message. Those temperamentally so inclined will find reassurance in two books we have already quoted, *The Way We Talk Now,* by Geoffrey Nunberg, and *Language Myths,* edited by Laurie Bauer and Peter Trudgill, a collection of essays debunking widely held conceptions (or, as the authors maintain, misconceptions) about our language.

Today, John Simon, aging gracefully with his Old World manners and faint accent, is a warrior unbowed, still willing to unsheathe his sword, as he did for us. Our conversation took place in the balcony of one of the Broadway theaters he frequents professionally, while, below, stagehands moved scenery for a new show, with the roar of New York traffic muted in the distance.

Simon believes American English has gotten worse in the quarter of a century since his book. "Our schools are not doing what they're supposed to do, they're not teaching us grammar or good usage. . . . Teachers in many cases don't know; and in any case they're lazy and they don't make enough corrections on papers." He went on to blame the media, political correctness, and descriptivist linguists, whom he called "a curse on their race, who of course think that what the people say is the law. I think a society in which the uneducated lead the educated by the nose is not a good society."

Jesse Sheidlower stands for all that John Simon hates. Sheidlower is the young Brooklyn-born American editor of the *Oxford English Dictionary* and a descriptivist linguist. Thin, bespectacled, wearing a dark suit and conservative tie, Sheidlower hardly looks like a champion of informality or permissiveness, yet he is the author of a scholarly book on the history of the word *fuck*. And he presides over the American contributions to a dictionary that embraces the most racy and up-to-the-minute expressions, if they have sufficient currency. Recent additions have included *blamestorming, churn rate,* and *fistfuck.* "We have a program at the *OED* devoted just to new words," he says. Apparently there is a group of editorial workers at the *OED* who do nothing but search for new words that have recently entered the language. Sheidlower gives the word *blog* as an example: "*Blog* is one of the newest, referring to Web logs or online journals, and all of the related terms, *blogging, blogger. In-*

tranet for an internet that's private to a company. We have older terms that missed out of the *OED* because they weren't paying that much attention to Americanisms. So, for example, the *disabled list* in baseball." Some others Sheidlower mentioned were *transgender* and *transgendered*, and *politically correct* words such as *lookism* and *sexism*. He noted, incidentally, that the term *politically correct* itself goes back to the late eighteenth century, where it is found in a Supreme Court decision. With our TV background, we noticed that the *OED* in 2003 adopted the word *magstripe*, meaning to apply a magnetic stripe to film to record sound, a term common in television since the 1960s.

Does Sheidlower believe that the language is being ruined by the great informality of American life? "No, it's not being ruined at all," he says. "The language is what it is." Sheidlower does not like to talk about "mistakes or carelessness." He prefers to speak of "more informal usages." In Sheidlower's view, people have always spoken informally, but today this informal language is beginning to appear in printed form and publications, where it would never have been seen in the past.

Sheidlower denies Simon's charge that they are regarding as law whatever ordinary people say. "Absolutely untrue," he says. "In fact, it's still the case that what the *educated* say is the law, because a language feature used only by the uneducated would always be described as just that." What Sheidlower means is that his dictionary makes the distinction between what is accepted as correct usage and what is still seen as "slang" or "informal." Sheidlower is also an authority on slang, first as project editor, now as consultant to the authoritative *Historical Dictionary of American Slang.*

But dictionary references and usage notes do evolve. Take the common American expression *come clean*, to tell or confess everything, which originated in cant, or underworld jargon, and emerged as common slang in the 1920s. In 1987, even the *Random House Dictionary*, which Simon thought so permissive, labeled *come clean* as "slang," but by 2001, for the *New Oxford American Dictionary*, it had become merely "informal." By January 2004, the Associated Press deemed it acceptable for a news story about Pete Rose: "More than a year before he *came clean* publicly in his new autobiography, Pete Rose told a high school newspaper that he bet on baseball."

Sheidlower thinks that John Simon and others who believe that there is a serious decline in linguistic standards are "wrong and misguided," because "language change happens and there's nothing you can do about it."

To which Simon replies, "Maybe change is inevitable . . . , maybe dying from cancer is also inevitable, but I don't think we should help it along."

We met Sheidlower at the main branch of the New York Public Library, at Fifth Avenue and Forty-second Street, where he often goes to look for new words and expressions. On that day he was examining magazines. "We try to find magazines that have words in them that we think are going to be of interest, and these can be in really any field out there." When we met him, he was looking at magazines related to tattooing, body piercing, and pop music: "There are terms for these different kinds of piercing and there are terms for different tattoos. *Blue Music* magazine has a lot of stuff about hip-hop, which has a big influence on the language."

When he finds a new word in one of these rather lurid magazines, does that mean that the dictionary will adopt, or recognize, the word? "No, not at all. For now it just means that we have an example in the database." The status of such a word begins to change when it makes a first appearance in a general-circulation magazine such as *Newsweek* or *New York*: "And we start to think, Well, okay, this is a term that started off as a very restricted, subcultural thing, but now it's widespread." Sheidlower and his colleagues force themselves to read magazines whose interest is, to put it mildly, highly specialized, because this is where new words will initially appear. This process teaches the *OED*'s dictionary writers "something that we wouldn't know if all we read was *Newsweek.*"

To Simon's complaint that the dictionary is too "permissive," the editor responds that this is a common mistake: "The purpose of the *Oxford English Dictionary* is not to tell people how to use language. . . . Putting a word into the *OED* doesn't make it an official part of English, or an approved part of English. Our purpose is to show how the language is being used." No matter that some of these new words may be slang, may be obscene, may be ethnically offensive. "Our purpose is not to say . . . 'We can't put those words in, they're not good words.' "

Sheidlower says that written English in America has been evolving greatly over the last hundred years, and especially in the last thirty or forty. "Nowadays, if you look at even the most formal publications, things like *The New Yorker* or the *New York Times,* you will find a wide variety of colloquial or slangy language used even in news articles. People speak this way and want to reflect this in their writing. Written English has become much more informal than it ever used to be."

Looking at the *New York Times* through Sheidlower's eyes did reveal the kind of language he described, with the stamp of contemporary informality and relaxed grammar. Some examples: "While the national *media is* roaring through Iowa" (accepting *media* as singular, which is now common); "But that process looked *like* it was going to take a year or two" (*like* in place of the *as if* or *as though* preferred by usage guides).

These are the kinds of usage that annoy the prescriptivists like John Simon, who took us through a list of his own pet peeves.

Like I said—"The word *as* has practically died out of English. It's *as I said,* not *like I said.* It's like underarm odor. I mean, you can live with it if the other person has it, but it's much nicer not to have to."

Media and *criteria*—"which are plural, but people don't know that because they haven't been taught properly and they think there's *a media* or *a criteria,* but there isn't. There's *a medium* and *a criterion.*"

It's not so big of a deal—"That's totally unnecessary and it's a sort of garbage word that just crept in there."

Masterful and *masterly*—"two very different words. A masterful person is a dominant, domineering person, but a masterly piece of work is masterly."

Between you and I—"which is all over the place, which Fowler called a genteelism, because people think that *I* is better than *me*."

Disinterested and *uninterested*—"two very different words, and they should not be confused," the first meaning *unprejudiced*, the second *not interested*.

I'm trying to get something off of my parents—"Why the second *of*? I'm trying to jump off the roof, not off of the roof."

Who and *whom*—"Even the worthy *New York Times* gets that terribly wrong. It's not too bad if you say *who* for *whom*. But it's terrible if you say *whom* for *who*. *The man whom is my father*—that's ugly."

Hopefully—"There's the one where even the conservatives are beginning to give way. But it doesn't make any sense. I mean, *hopefully, mercifully*, anything that has *-fully* in it means that we need a vessel that is filled with this hope or this mercy. To say, *Hopefully it won't rain tomorrow*, who or what is filled with hope? Nothing. So you have to say, *I hope it won't rain tomorrow*. But you can say, *I enter a room hopefully*, because you are the vessel for that hopefulness."

Descripivists see these changes as all part of the organic growth of American English and of the language generally, as it has always grown. Thus the erosion of foreign plurals in words such as *media* and *criteria* is typical of the long development of English and is nothing to worry about. And *hopefully* is no different from *thankfully* or *mercifully*, which we have long accepted.

Modern computer technology, which makes it possible to scan and search through complete texts going back hundreds of years, casts a new light on this long-running debate: "We see that *hopefully* is not in fact very new, as people thought it was in the 1960s," Sheidlower says.

"It goes back hundreds of years, and it has been very common even in highly educated speech for much of that time. You find it in the twentieth century very commonly in academic journals."

Why, then, do people suddenly get so upset about it now?

Sheidlower: "Because they were told to be upset. Their teachers, you know, language conservatives, say that this is wrong and this is right, and they grow up thinking that, and often when there's no historical basis for it."

He instanced the "alleged distinction" between *masterly* and *masterful*. "This distinction never existed in language until Henry Fowler said it did in 1926. It was just completely an invention. There is no basis for it whatsoever, but now people think that it is a real distinction and anyone who says this is wrong."

Sheidlower maintains that John Simon sees language through a kind of middle- or upper-class prism, which means really taking an elitist view. He maintains that people like John Simon are actually complaining that linguists and dictionary writers are no longer focused exclusively on the language of top people: "When linguistic conservatives look at the way things were in the old days and say, 'Well, everything used to be very proper, and now we have all these bad words and people are being careless and so forth,' in fact people always used to be that way," Sheidlower says. "It's just that you didn't hear them, because the media would only report on the language of the educated upper middle class. Nowadays . . . we see the language of other groups, of other social groups, of other income levels in a way that we never used to. And the two world wars have had a very big effect on this. You take people from all sorts of different places and all sorts of different backgrounds and throw them together, and you have a tremendous blending of language that had a very big effect on how people speak."

That people are no longer bothering about the distinction between *uninterested* and *disinterested* "doesn't really matter in the long run," Sheidlower believes. "You can tell usually by context what the differences are.

A very small number of words have distinctions like this. I don't think there's a distinction between *disinterested* and *uninterested,* which by the way is a very modern distinction. For most of the history of these two words they were used interchangeably, and only relatively recently did someone say *disinterested* means one thing and *uninterested* means another. You know, it doesn't really matter."

John Simon is perfectly happy to be called an elitist, regretting that it has become a pejorative word: "All it means is making good choices. And there is nothing wrong with making good choices: to eat at a good restaurant or a bad one, to drive a good car rather than a bad car. And, in the same way, to use words that are more correct, more precise, more correctly evocative of what you're trying to say. If that is elitist, well, perhaps it is, and in that case, I'm very happy to be an elitist. There is such a thing as beautiful behavior and ugly behavior, and that goes for language as well as for not breaking wind in public."

Does Simon think America no longer cares about language? "Yes, that's true. And, of course, it's the general devaluation. I mean, a society in which Maya Angelou can be thought to be a real poet of some importance is a doomed society. I mean, that is trash. . . . I think there ought to be some kind of public . . . protest against vulgarity, against bad usage, against bad manners, against the uneducated dictating to the educated. It's not an easy proposition, I grant. It's a matter of standards. It's a matter of one aspiring to be a gentleman, for example, or a gentlewoman. And now one doesn't aspire to that anymore."

Of course, we are not going to resolve this dispute, but there is one interesting footnote. Noting that databases can now be searched for texts hundreds of years old, writer John Rosenthal believes computers are giving descriptivists an advantage:

> For years when it came to settling language disputes, the prescriptivists have held the upper hand. Their thick volumes con-

tained unequivocal rules of grammar, which they could look up at any time. Descriptivists, meanwhile, typically have had to reply on what "sounds" more natural. . . . But with the advent of the computer, the balance of power is shifting. That's because the computer makes it infinitely easier to track patterns of English usage and catalogue them for use as reference material. Finally, the descriptivists have an empirical source of verbal ammunition: concrete examples of how the language is actually used.

A consortium of publishers, software companies, and academics, including Pearson, Microsoft, Sony, and the Universities of California, Colorado, and Pennsylvania, among many others, is now creating the American National Corpus. When completed, with a hundred million words in its database, Rosenthal says, "It will provide a definitive portrait of how the English language is used in the United States today."

As in many political arguments, the rhetoric of the public figures in the language wars probably fires up the activists but must leave many people feeling somewhere in the middle. Most of us who care about the language are bound to harbor some prescriptivist sentiment and some descriptivist.

Where one fits on the prescriptivist/descriptivist spectrum is probably determined by many factors, including education, temperament, and general outlook on life—and age. We wouldn't be human if we didn't, especially as we grow older, regret the disappearance of things we cherish—certain music, buildings, and niceties of language. On the other hand, it is not only human but very American to delight in novelty, and our language bursts with it. The freedom and inventiveness of American usage reminds some linguists of how the English language was in Shakespeare's day.

Here are some freshly minted American usages encountered in New

York City: After defeating spray-painted *graffiti,* the subway system found artists scratching the windows and put up new signs: *No scratchiti.* Two terms borrowed from TV and film: "She is *fastforwarding* the place" and "She's still getting dressed. It's a *slo-mo* day" (from *slow motion*). A man who had enough of a friendship: "I *bitter-ended* it." CNN newscaster Aaron Brown to an interviewee: "I am *shorthanding* this, obviously." After researching someone online: "I *Googled* you." A fashion designer: "It's so *dope*! It's going to be everywhere!" Clyde Haberman of the *New York Times* in a column about the people of 2003: "its most laudable figures and vilest *sleazoids.*" A girl in an elevator to a young man: "You're cute. What's your *mix?*" (racial mix). A Citibank billboard: "You were born to be *preapproved.*" *Nimbyism* (Not in My Backyard–ism) is resistance to unwelcome development in a neighborhood. Jeff MacGregor writing in the *New York Times* described himself: "I, sophisticated *sarcast,* turn to NASCAR dad . . ." John Lahr, in *The New Yorker:* "When he finally appears in full tropical suit *suavicity* . . ."

What is it about America that promotes so much change in language? One factor important to Jesse Sheidlower is that "American English has always been very inclusive of new terms. We have a great deal of immigration from around the world. . . . So terms from all the different cultures, or from different ethnic groups, or from different social groups, have a way of getting into the language in a way that you don't see because of the cultural mixing that we have here. . . . I think American English very exciting compared to other languages around the world."

One could speculate that living and working in big immigrant cities like New York, with neighbors and colleagues who spoke anything but correct or fluent English, may have made Americans more tolerant of divergent forms of speech, at least as a source of humor. Whatever the cause, speakers of American English have always leaned toward the informal.

The more relaxed American attitude was naturally reflected on

Madison Avenue, with verbal informalities such as *Winston tastes good like a cigarette should* becoming so much a part of the culture that linguists now doubt that many Americans today would notice the grammatical lapse. Advertisers were as quick as politicians to meet average Americans on a comfortable linguistic level. President George W. Bush became the butt of many jokes when he said, "There's no negotiations with North Korea." But in casual speech most Americans don't bother about subject-verb agreement when beginning sentences with *there is,* just as Mr. Bush fits the increasingly common way of dropping "g"s to sound friendly, as in *Howya doin'? Doin' great!*

Social hierarchies have always been much weaker in the United States than in older countries. One of the attractions of America from the earliest days was that colonists could throw off their predetermined status in the Old World order, which condemned them for life to the social rank and profession to which they were born. From the beginning, America was a culture in which you could, were almost expected to, reinvent yourself, with whatever that meant in adopting new language.

There is great social mobility, Americans traditionally aspiring to move up the social ladder and adopting, or at least seeing their children adopt, whatever language norms the new level requires. Perversely perhaps, the current younger generation tends toward a "subversive prestige" or "covert prestige," as linguists put it, in adopting the speech of less privileged minorities; for instance, *wiggers* are privileged white teenagers who wish to sound and dress like blacks.

Youth in general, teenagers in particular, delight in setting themselves and friends apart with their own slang, and this is a culture obsessively deferential to youth. Geoffrey Nunberg marvels that high-school graduates in 2003 "have never known what it is to be young in an era when older people didn't hang on their every word." His observation was inspired by an article in *The New Yorker* about young marketing consultants who took corporate clients on guided tours of the youth culture in New York's outer boroughs to pick up the latest slang. As people got older, they used to grow out of their youthful slang and start deploring the language of the next generation. Now the tastes and desires of teenagers drive such an enormous consumer market that their language becomes a tool in advertising the movies, the clothes, the makeup, the magazines, and the music they like.

Another factor in changing our language is a quality every visitor to America notices: speed. Americans are in a hurry, especially in New York. A cartoon in *The New Yorker* several years ago showed many people walking rapidly, bent forward, and only one person upright. A person behind him says, "Walk faster, this is New York!" You might say, "Talk faster, this is New York."

On television, as time became more valuable, commercials shorter, and the programs between the commercials faster-paced, it has been remarked that news programs are leaving out verbs, or using mostly present participles, in a new, abbreviated language; for example, John King on CNN: "Those negotiations continuing. Mr. Bush speaking to reporters earlier today. Suddenly optimistic."

Shepard Smith, news anchor on the Fox News Channel, says, "You sort of eliminate the things that get in your way in this era of multitasking, and sometimes verbs just aren't necessary. It's 'President Bush in Washington today.' I don't need to say, 'He is in Washington today.' We're telling more stories in our hour than any national newscast in the history of this business, I think . . . and sometimes verbs just get in the way."

Tom Phillips was a script doctor for years at CBS News. He says that twenty years ago "we had the feeling we were writing for an audience of twelve-year-olds." Whom were they writing for now? "I think maybe a seven-year-old."

Or as Geoffrey Nunberg put it, considering twenty-four-hour cable: "The news getting hard to pin down these days, it seeming. News becoming more like life, just one damn thing after another."

These are some of the explanations of why American society generates so much new language and so many changes in existing English. It is a restless, innovative society, its social patterns and mores, its *lifestyles*, evolving as swiftly as its genius in scientific and technological creativity; it is endlessly inventive in finding new pathways for the pursuit of happiness and marketing them to an American population approaching three hundred million. All that activity makes language change.

But there are more mysterious, underground forces at work, still imperfectly understood, driving broader and perhaps deeper changes in the American language.

two

Changing Dialects: Dingbatters Versus Hoi-Toiders

Many Americans believe that television and radio are homogenizing our language, making all of us talk more alike. To linguists that is a myth. Despite decades in which we have listened to or watched the same programs, the regional differences in American speech remain vigorous. Paradoxically, the truth seems to be that, where change occurs, it is often creating more diversity, not less. Some dialects are indeed threatened with extinction; this is, however, caused not by the media but by movements of people.

Someone once observed that if you traveled down the Atlantic coast of the United States you would hear dozens of distinctive local dialects, but if you drove straight west across the country you would hear just one. This is an oversimplification, but it holds a lot of truth, because there is more dialect diversity in the East than in the West.

The veteran Broadway actor Jerry Orbach, now internationally famous for his role in the TV series *Law and Order*, describes how he was taught the basics of regional accents in an elocution class at Northwestern University. The future actors were given a shorthand key to East Coast accents, using the phrase *stark naked*. In Boston and the Northeast, it would be *stack naked;* in New York City, *stock naked;* and in Georgia and the Southeast, *stalk naked*.

South Freeport is a small town on the coast of Maine, up the Harraseeket River, sheltered from the storms of the North Atlantic in one of the hundreds of deep inlets that make this shoreline so photogenic and so hospitable to seafarers. After a drive along the foggy coastline, we found John Coffin at the dock, unloading freshly caught lobsters, green-black before the cooking that turns them red. Coffins have lived here for generations, as the town thrived on fishing and shipbuilding. A ruggedly handsome man in his late sixties, John himself has been lobstering for more than forty years. He notices that two things central to his life are changing.

In recent years, the lobsters have been getting scarcer around his part of the coast, and he hears less and less of the Down East speech he grew up with and still speaks. (*Down East* derives from sailing days, when going east usually meant sailing *downwind*.) He says, "I listen to all the little kids that hang around my grandchildren and I don't hear it. I think it must be their parents don't talk it." Their parents may be among the many new people who have moved into the area, so many that John says, "I can walk around town all day long and I won't see a handful of people I know." The larger town of Freeport (*up the road apiece,* as locals would say) used to be the modest headquarters of the clothing store L. L. Bean, but has morphed into a mega–outlet center for many other firms, its population swelled by their employees and customers. Today, newcomers commute from homes on the coast here to jobs in Portland or even Boston.

As for the local dialect—or accent, as John Coffin would call it—with its characteristic *ayuh* for *yes,* "I think in this area it's going to be a lost thing. I think they're trying to get away from it here," and that makes him sad. "I'd like to think my children and grandchildren talk that way, whether people laugh at you, wherever we go—whatever." Do they laugh at the Maine accent? "Oh yes, lots of times. When I was in the military, they made fun of me *wicked.*" *Wicked* is a characteristic Maine word, meaning *very,* often combined, as in *wicked good, wicked bad,* or *wicked exciting*. Some other local dialect words are *cunnin'* for cute, *numb* for stupid, as in *numb as a hake*, and *from away* for anyone not from Maine. But most noticeable to outsiders is the pronunciation, leaving out the "r" sound after vowels and making two syllables of some words, so that *there* and *here* become *they-uh* and *hee-ah*. The "a" sound is broadened so that *bath* becomes *bahth*, and *can't* sounds like *cahn't*. It's the accent that Angela Lansbury and fellow actors were aiming for in the TV series *Murder, She Wrote*.

John Coffin probably speaks for many Americans who see their small, traditional communities flooded by newcomers and feel their way of speech evaporating, along with part of what identifies them and where they belong.

The Maine way of talking is part of a larger speech pattern centered on Boston, known as the Eastern New England dialect. It is one of the "r"-less speech patterns deriving from some of the earliest English settlers, who did not pronounce the "r" in words like *father*. If his local speech is threatened with extinction, as John Coffin's ears tell him, then it would join others from isolated East Coast communities overrun by new people. Local dialects thrive when communities are isolated, which is how different dialects, even whole languages, evolved in the first place. When many outsiders move in, the local speech usually changes.

A number of island dialects on the eastern seaboard are in grave danger of extinction. No longer self-sustaining communities, these islands are now service-based tourist meccas, often expanded by developments of expensive second homes for people from other states.

The island of Edisto, off the South Carolina coast, is an example. In the 1980s, a few elderly people still spoke Gullah, a dialect linguists trace back to the African slave trade. Twenty years later, Gullah has ceased to be a naturally spoken language but is kept going artificially by some as a cultural artifact and a tourist attraction.

The dialect on the island of Ocracoke, off the coast of North Carolina, about fifty miles south of Roanoke Island, site of the first British attempt to create a colony in America, is dying out because many outsiders have moved in, diluting native speech with their own. Sometimes referred to as the Outer Banks Brogue, Ocracoke dialect is marked by unusual pronunciations of words like *high* and *tide,* which sound like *hoi* and *toid,* so that locals are often referred to as *Hoi-Toiders.* That is in pretty sharp contrast to *tahm* or *tahd,* which is how *time* and *tide* are said by Southerners who live inland in North Carolina.

For generations they had that vowel sound in common with New Yorkers, the traditional "oy" sound often ridiculed in the pronunciation of *Thirty-third and Third* as *Toity-toid and Toid.* It is now rare to find it in the speech of New Yorkers born after World War II.

There is one sense in which Ocracokers have been affected by television. They have borrowed *dingbat,* Archie Bunker's insulting name for his wife, Edith, in the 1970s television series *All in the Family.* Islanders call outsiders *dingbatters.*

In contrast to this, dialects in some island communities are getting stronger and more distinctive, because they have not been overrun by *dingbatters.* Maryland's Smith Island, in the Chesapeake Bay, was settled in the late seventeenth century by people originally from southwestern England. The 360 people who make a living harvesting soft-shell crabs have preserved expressions such as *of a winter,* as in *We go ice-skating of a winter,* and *of a night,* as in *We used to visit our neighbors of a night.*

But, like lobsters in Maine, crabs are getting scarce, the island is losing population, and there is increasing contact with the outside world— all a common recipe for *dialect dissipation,* as the linguists call it. Instead, the opposite is happening and is known as *dialect concentration.* Some distinctive expressions have been on the rise—for example, the use of *weren't* for the past tense in negative sentences regardless of subject person or number, such as *It weren't me, She weren't home.* In Ocracoke the same use is disappearing, but on Smith Island it is growing.

There are several possible reasons. One is the concentration of population in a small area, with a new high school that permits teenagers to stay on the island instead of boarding on the mainland all week. Also, Smith Islanders consider their dialect an important part of their cultural uniqueness, a badge of their independence and distinctiveness. Smith Island's dialect is close to that on nearby Tangier Island, Virginia, so close that their common name for each other is *yarney*, derived from *yarnin'*, or telling tales. Smith Island is one of the many places it's claimed that Elizabethan or Shakespearean English survives. Linguists regard this as a hoary myth, because the "old-time" words or expressions offered as evidence do not add up to what is claimed.

But the myth persists. Walt Wolfram tells the story of a BBC television producer who came determined to film "Shakespearean" English spoken on Ocracoke, and approached Wolfram as the acknowledged expert on the local dialect. The linguist told the producer he was barking up the wrong tree, but he wouldn't take no for an answer. Wolfram later found him filming a resident of the island reading aloud a passage from Shakespeare, the producer complaining that he didn't sound "Shakespearean" enough.

Changing How Dialects Are Studied

The earliest dialect studies looked for words particular to one region and drew lines to connect similarities of usage. From those findings, they produced the first dialect maps. This work continues in the mammoth undertaking begun by Frederic G. Cassidy in the *Dictionary of American Regional English,* known familiarly as *DARE,* of which four of the five projected volumes have been published. Yet many area-specific words are disappearing. Modern communications and changing employment patterns have been eroding the odd words people used very locally for activities like farming—or crab fishing on Smith Island. Old craft skills have been rendered extinct by products marketed nationally, so that local words for the local crafts die out with each generation that used them.

Linguist Guy Bailey said that, before World War II, regional varieties of American English differed in folk vocabularies: "I'll give you an example. I grew up in south Alabama, and the name I had for *dragonfly* was *mosquito hog.* We use the term *gopher* for a large land turtle that made holes, and rattlesnakes lived down in *gopher* holes." Bailey said that much of the folk vocabulary has already gone, partly "because we make a living pretty much the same around the country now."

Some regional vocabulary survives for things still in use. What most of the country calls a *milk shake* is still a *frappe* in Massachusetts. In different regions the same carbonated beverage is known variously as *soda, pop, tonic, soft drink,* or generically, whatever the flavor, *a Coke.* Differences survive in names for a long sandwich containing cold cuts, cheese, and lettuce. It is known as a *grinder* chiefly in New England; a *wedge* in Rhode Island and coastal Connecticut; a *spuky* in Boston; a *hero* (occasionally a *torpedo*) in New York; a *hoagie* in Philadelphia; a *submarine* in Ohio and farther west. But many of these terms have spread widely, so they are no longer strictly regional markers.

More recently, linguists began marking dialect areas not by different vocabulary but by how differently words were pronounced. The *Atlas of North American English* is based on phone calls to randomly selected people all over the United States and Canada. They are asked how they pronounce a list of words, and their different pronunciations are marked by colored dots. Clusters of similarly colored dots define a dialect area but also show how pronunciations from a neighboring area can infiltrate or bleed into it—for example, how the typically Southern pronunciation of *I* (a single syllable resembling *Ah*) pops up in states north of the Mason-Dixon Line, where the usual pronunciation makes *I* sound more like two syllables, *Eye-ee*. The map is going to be available on the Internet, so that visitors to the Web site can choose a word from the test list, then click on the colored dots and hear how that word is said in their hometown or elsewhere.

The dialect areas revealed by the new phonological approach, mapping by pronunciations, still correspond closely with the old dialect mapping by local word use, as shown, for example, in the comprehensive *Dictionary of American Regional English*. Linguists are impressed by how stable the traditional boundaries remain, between North, Midland, and South dialect regions, even with all the modern movement of people. Walt Wolfram says, "The first group to settle an area seems to have a lasting effect on the dialect area. And even though we've got all these changes over a couple of hundred years, the original dialect boundaries seem to be fairly intact still." The same boundaries, interestingly, also correspond with traces of the different styles of architecture that the original settlers adopted—whether they built frame houses, stone houses, or log cabins.

What the new technique does reveal for the first time, however, is how language is changing.

One of the leading scholars in the field is William Labov, of the University of Pennsylvania, director of the *Atlas of North American English* and author of a series of books on how language changes and why.

Recent research appears to show very little change in syntax, the grammatical structure of American English, although some regional markers—like the Southern *fixin' to*, as in *I'm fixin' to go to town*—can become more common as population shifts to the Sun Belt and newly arrived Northerners want to blend in. So it is on pronunciation that linguists have focused their search for change and its causes.

Labov believes there are startling and powerful changes taking place in how American English is pronounced—some regional, some sweeping across the whole nation. One nationwide trend is the tendency to pronounce the vowel in the word *do* more like the sound in *dew*. He calls it *oo-fronting:* "Americans used to say *ou* just like the French *vous*. That's almost gone. Only in one or two cities can you still find *ou*. What you get is a vowel that starts much fronter in the mouth. And it sounds like *ew* in the most extreme form." By that change, *you* sounds like *yew*. Another is the habit among younger speakers of putting a rising inflection at the end of positive statements that would normally conclude with a falling voice, so that a sentence such as *I'm the new secretary* sounds like *I'm the new secretary?*—a question, not a statement. That is believed to have spread from California, not just across the United States but around the English-speaking world. In the 1980s, in *The Story of English,* we found it in Australia.

There are startling vowel changes in the largest American dialect areas, North and South. In the North, the most dramatic change involves about thirty-four million people in cities around the Great Lakes—Chicago, Syracuse, Rochester, Cleveland, and Detroit—the area Labov calls Inland North. What began in these cities in the mid-twentieth century is now spreading into rural areas.

Labov has dramatic examples. On the computer in his Philadelphia office, you hear a woman say *black*, then the whole phrase "Old senior citizens living on one *black*," and from the context you realize she says *block* like *black*. Another woman mentions *bosses*, but the full sentence is "I can vaguely remember when we had the *bosses* with the antennas on top." She is making *buses* sound like *bosses*. In other examples, *dot* becomes *dat, socks* turns into *sacks*. Labov calls this phenomenon the Northern Cities Shift, "a revolutionary change in the pronunciation of short vowels that otherwise have been relatively stable in English for a thousand years."

When one vowel changes, it has a kind of domino effect on the others. As Matthew Gordon, of the University of Missouri–Columbia, puts it, "One vowel shifts into the space of a neighboring vowel. The contrast between the vowels is maintained, however, because that neighboring vowel also shifts. For example, *caught* shifts toward *cot*, *cot* shifts toward *cat*, and *cat* shifts toward *kit* or 'keeyat.'"

This change is so extraordinary that it merits another example, provided by one of Labov's colleagues, linguist Sharon Ash: the vowel sound in *tock* shifts to *tack*, *tack* to *tech*, *tech* to *tuck*, *tuck* to *talk*, and *talk* back to *tock*. Ash says, "There is only so much room in the mouth," so that when one vowel shifts, the others have to shift to another part of the mouth.

Labov believes this vowel change is "terribly" important: "From our point of view as linguists we want to understand why people should become more different from each other. We're all watching the same radio and television, we live side by side. And it's important to recognize that people don't always want to behave in the same way. These dialect differences are the major reasons why computers cannot understand people. . . . Now, we don't know yet what's driving the whole engine, but we know it's the same forces that have led to this tremendous dispersion of our language family. So at one time Hindi and Albanian and Russian and Greek and German were the same language."

Labov is referring to the lost parent language of the Indo-European family, from which many modern languages evolved. He is thus equating—rather dramatically—the forces of dispersal, isolation, and local identity working on our language today with the same human forces and the same language needs acting eons ago, which produced many different languages, and later produced French, Italian, Spanish, and Portuguese out of Latin. "Hard to believe, because we all watch the same television—how can that be?" Labov says, "It's a very surprising finding."

Such vowel shifts have happened in other places—in England, for example, where the broad "a" has moved back and forth several times—but it is too early to predict what will happen in the Northern Cities Shift. Labov believes it is not likely that the whole rotation will be reversed.

Equally dramatic changes are happening to language in the South (there is a Southern Shift in vowels as well) and to African American English, and we will be getting to both later.

Some of the sound changes observed in Philadelphia are quite radical, and often cause misunderstandings. Consider this conversation in 1990 between a mother (not a Philadelphian) and her daughter, who had picked up the changed vowel that made *eight* sound like *eat*.

MOTHER: Do you want me to cut up your pizza for you?
GIRL: Mom, I'm eight!
MOTHER: I know you're *eating*, but . . .
GIRL: Mom, I'm *eight*!

Another anecdote involves a shift in the vowel in the word *slaves* to the vowel in *leave*. It was supper time for a South Philadelphia family:

WIFE: Okay, time to eat!
LABOV: You run a tight ship.
HUSBAND: She makes us *slaves*.
WIFE: Why would I want you to *leave*?

What Causes Such Change?

Where does such change begin, and what or who actually causes it? One theory is that it is driven by women.

Labov argues that women have been both the primary transmitters of language and more sensitive to language than men; traditionally having less economic power, they relied on the symbolic control offered by words. Women are quicker than men to adopt "prestige forms" of language, but also quicker to adopt symbols of nonconformism, new or "stigmatized forms" that can acquire a kind of "covert prestige." Labov writes that "women perceive and react to prestige or stigma more strongly than men do, and when change begins, women are quicker and more forceful in employing the new social symbolism, whatever it may be."

One of the first to notice this was a French dialectician, Louis Gauchat, who studied changing pronunciations in the dialect of a small village in the Swiss Alps. In a number of vowel changes, women were a generation ahead of their husbands. Gauchat explained this by noting that the men were out in the fields all day with no one to talk to, while the women talked all day long.

In Philadelphia, Labov identified a particular type of woman, working-class, well established in her community, who took pleasure in being non-conformist and was strong enough to influence others. As an adolescent she resisted adult authority, particularly when it was perceived as unjust, but stayed on an upwardly mobile path in the social structure. Labov says that these leaders of linguistic change have had a history of nonconformity and that their language itself was a display of nonconformity.

A good example was Celeste S., a pseudonym for the leading figure among a group of residents of Clark Street, a pseudonym for a real street in South Central Philadelphia. She had grown up in a second-generation Sicilian family in which her father, a shoemaker, was a fierce and domineering presence. As a teenager at the end of World War II, Celeste resisted him:

> I used to go to the movies and she [her mother] used to send a couple of boys up the street to watch who I used to be in the movies with. But we were in cahoots, the boys and I. That's the only way you could get out—like we'd date. I would date. And like . . . my father would say, "Where you goin'?" "Well, daddy, now look! Georgie's gonna take me—George down the street." And daddy thought, "Oh, boy, she's safe with Georgie." So Georgie would go *his* way and I would go *my* way. And then we

would meet, see, at a certain time . . . and we'd come home like
two nice little kids.

Eventually Celeste married a skilled draftsman and became a highly
respected figure on one of the most prosperous blocks in South Philadelphia. She was the one who went door to door collecting money for flowers or a mass card when someone on the block died, or who organized
the block effort in putting up Christmas lights. She was never afraid to
speak her mind bluntly, as on the day when she heard that the priest
had failed to write a letter requesting that a local boy in the service be
granted leave to visit his mother, who was dying of cancer. Celeste
marched into the rectory, where the priest was eating lunch, and said,
"You son of a gun! You don't have time to write a letter for a dying
woman!" He jumped up and said, "Celeste, I was just going to write it."
In telling the story, Celeste said, "I usually call him a baldheaded bas-
tard, but I wasn't going to do it to him then."

She was the kind of woman to whom people looked as a point of reference, and who was likely to influence their actions and opinions. Linguistically she showed new and vigorous changes. In two vowels in
particular, Celeste's pronunciations showed the most advanced changes
in her community: her pronunciation of *house* moved towards *hess, mouth*
sounded like *meth,* and *south* like *seth.* The vowel in *name* moved toward
neem, in *made* toward *mead.*

Labov sees surprising parallels between leadership in fashion and
language change. Young women are always alert to novelty in fashion,
but certain young women are willing to embrace it sooner, and some
have the natural authority to induce others to follow. "Fashion leaders
are concentrated among young women of high gregariousness," Labov
says, calling the linguistic changes he has studied "the audible equiva-
lent of the visual effects of fashion."

Labov's theory has been elaborated in the research of Stanford University linguist Penelope Eckert, who studied language changes originating among high-school students in a predominantly white suburb of Detroit. Eckert's well-known study, published as *Jocks and Burnouts*, divided the high-school population into students who tended to conform to adult norms (Jocks) and those resisting adult authority (Burnouts). Females among the Burnouts were the principal leaders of linguistic change, measured by how completely they adopted the vowel changes in the Northern Cities Shift. However, the most advanced speakers were so-called brokers, students who transmitted information between Jocks and Burnouts, and whose status in school was defined largely by verbal activity in gossip and negotiation.

Labov told us: "We're just speculating that there are certain people who pick up symbols of social nonconformity and they keep it all their lives and even promote it. But they don't remain outside society. On the contrary, they are people who move right up into the strongest social positions. And they bring with them these symbols of nonconformity that gradually spread to the entire community." He still finds it mysterious.

J. K. Chambers of the University of Toronto says that changes themselves are usually crystal-clear—for example, the trend he's studied in Canada and Northern American states to replace *dived* as the past-tense form by *dove*. But the reasons behind the change are much more difficult to pinpoint, the number of possibilities enormous. They include "adolescent rebellion from childhood norms, grammatical fine tuning by young adults making their way in the marketplace, fads, fancies and fashions, and much more. All these things operate beneath consciousness, of course, making their detection even harder. You cannot see them or measure them; you can only infer them."

Another Factor: Local Pride and Identity

So—mysterious forces within society, operating beneath consciousness, are driving significant language change, making Americans from one region harder for others to understand at a time when other mass trends in our society are toward conformity.

Dennis Baron, of the University of Illinois at Urbana-Champaign, sees interplay between the global and local forces. As American English stretches around the world to become close to universal as a second or a third language, there seems to be a corresponding reinforcing of the local variety.

People in St. Louis, for example, continue to merge the sound "ahr" in words such as *car, are, far* with the "ohr" sound found in *corps, or, for*—strong enough to be a defining feature of a St. Louis dialect.

People in Louisville, Kentucky, still say *my shoes need shined, my clothes want washed.* Linguist Dennis Preston says, "It's completely ungrammatical to me, and yet I grew up around Louisville, only a few miles south of the area where that's perfectly grammatical. But as soon as they move out and say something like, you know, *the car needs washed,* people around them look at them as if they're not native speakers of English."

In Pittsburgh, this local reinforcement through language has become highly self-conscious, a constant topic of conversation and regular features in the local press. Pittsburgh is Barbara Johnstone's hometown, and we stopped there to talk to her about it, while walking through the old market section of ethnic food stores and restaurants. In a time when some dialects are disappearing, the old coal-and-steel city is clinging to, even promoting, "Pittsburghese" as a mark of pride and local identity. It uses distinctive words like *yinz,* for the plural of *you,* or *you ones,* now such an identifier that some Pittsburghers refer to themselves as *Yinzers.* They use *slippy* for *slippery; red up* meaning *to tidy up; nebby,* an Old English word for *nosy;* and *anymore,* as in "*Anymore,* there's so many new buildings you can't tell which is which." Like people in Louisville, they say something needing repair *needs repaired*. These usages are delivered in an accent that is also considered distinctively Pittsburgh. *Downtown* is pronounced *dahntahn, wash* is *worsh*. *Did you eat yet?* comes out *Jeetjet?* And the reply, *No, jew?*

This Pittsburgh dialect has become a commodity in books and T-shirts. We stopped at one of the many stores selling souvenirs displaying Pittsburghese, the T-shirts bearing a glossary of local expressions. The manager of one said, "Oh yes, Pittsburgh language is big business." He sells three or four dozen in a good week, often to former Pittsburghers who are back for a visit. We asked him to translate the words on one of his T-shirts.

Art—"*Out,* opposite of *in.*"
Babushka—"Head scarf used for a bad-hair day."
Blitzberg—"Drinking town with a football team."
Chipteam—"Family-sliced ham sold only in the Burg."
Dahntahn—"Downtown. That's where you're at now."
Jag-off—"Anyone who pisses off a Pittsburgher."

What would do that? we asked. The T-shirt salesman said, "Just tell him the Steelers suck." The name of the football teams is pronounced *Stillers.*

Johnstone thinks this local accent, which is different from how people talk elsewhere, is really a way of identifying and affirming their place: they are talking about who they are and where they live and what it means to live here. In the context of globalization and people moving around, she says, "You often hear that places don't matter the way they used to." But this is completely wrong: people treasure their local accents, precisely because where they come from, or where they feel they belong, does still matter.

Although Pittsburgh carries the image of a place shaped by Eastern and Southern European immigrants, who poured into the great steel mills in the nineteenth century, its language was most strongly influenced by the Scots-Irish settlers (Ulstermen from Northern Ireland) who came a century earlier. There is speculation that the very spelling of the city's name, ending with an "h," echoed the Scottish *Edinburgh*, whereas *Harrisburg*, the state capital, like *Hamburg* with no "h," reflected the influence of many German settlers. When the Poles and Italians arrived in the Pittsburgh area, the local English they learned had deep Scots-Irish roots. Barbara Johnstone says many terms thought to be unique to Pittsburgh are not. What is local is not the word, such as the characteristic *yinz*, but what they think about it. It feeds a sense of local identity centered on the city—they tend to think of themselves in terms of the city rather than the region, since there doesn't seem to be a strong sense of being a Pennsylvanian the way Texans have a strong sense of being Texan.

So language feeds a local pride that has taken hard knocks as foreign competition killed the steel mills. The football team may still proudly call itself the Steelers, but the implications of the death of that bedrock industry for local society are reflected in attitudes toward language. In the old days, when most men worked in the steel mills, it didn't matter how they talked, Johnstone says, because each felt like one of the guys, but with employment now shifting to the service industries, the local dialect can work against them. "People have told me that they were told when they interviewed for a job, 'You would have gotten the job if you didn't have a local accent.'" Pittsburgh's women had to learn that sooner, because they moved earlier than men into office and service jobs.

Today, there are more and more jobs in which it matters how employees talk. People who work at a telephone call center have their accents monitored, and may be refused jobs because of regional accents. One of the reasons there are so many technical-support call centers in Ontario is that the Canadian accent is not perceived by Americans as regional.

That raises an interesting question about the burgeoning offshore call-center industry in Bangalore, India. The Indian employees are mostly college-educated and take pains, if not to sound American, to adopt certain American idioms and catchphrases acquired from watching TV sitcoms. The much lower Indian wages drive this growing offshore employment, but it is interesting that Indian voices are acceptable to many American customers, whereas certain homegrown regional accents might put them off.

The Effect of the Media

It is interesting that the vowel changes we have noted do not push the language toward pronunciations that fit within broadcast-media norms; in fact, some move radically away from them.

All this evidence contradicts the popular assumption that the mass media are homogenizing American English and causing its treasured local varieties to disappear. The linguists we interviewed believe that the media can be useful in spreading vocabulary and causing innovations to be picked up and spread faster. Media saturation may also provide what Dennis Baron called a "passive lingua franca." We all understand what we hear on the radio or see on TV, giving us a passive vocabulary, but that doesn't mean that we use that vocabulary actively in writing or speaking. Similarly, we can understand accents different from our own, but few people change their accents because of it. In fact, many Americans can be amusingly unaware of their own accents: linguists have collected many stories of people with strong local accents, in places like Texas and coastal North Carolina, who thought they talked like Walter Cronkite!

John Baugh, a Stanford linguist, believes that mainstream media dialect is well understood by speakers of American English from almost every background, but that media influence on actual speech patterns is not great, because those speech patterns are really shaped locally.

Carmen Fought summed it up succinctly. For all the media Americans consume—and the statistical averages put them in front of television alone more than four hours a day—"People want to talk like the people they want to be like."

three

Toward a Standard: Putting the "R" in "American"

In the rest of the English-speaking world, probably the most characteristic sound in American English is the fully sounded "r," known to linguists as the *postvocalic /r/*, the "r" following vowels. But it might not have been that way. Though some coastal settlers in Virginia and North Carolina brought their strong "r" from southwestern England, all but one of the big cultural and population centers in colonial America were settled predominantly by English people from areas where the "r" was not pronounced. Boston, New York, Richmond, Savannah, and Charleston were "r"-less. Philadelphia was the exception, the only East Coast city originally to pronounce its "r"s. It is possible that Philadelphia shaped American speech more than any other city, because the "r" sound that so typifies American English migrated west from Philadelphia. That makes Philadelphia not only the cradle of American independence, but the cradle of what we think of today as modern American language.

Philadelphia was different because of the heavy influx of Scots-Irish immigrants in the decades just before the American Revolution. They were Lowland Scots who had settled in Northern Ireland, where their Presbyterian faith brought them into conflict with the Catholic Irish and the Anglican English. By 1760, Benjamin Franklin, Philadelphia's most illustrious citizen, reckoned that Scots-Irish accounted for a third of the city population, with English and Germans each another third. George Washington said he could not have won the Revolutionary War without these tough and belligerent Ulstermen, who carried plenty of grievances against England.

In the 1720s, when they began migrating to America in large numbers, many landed in Philadelphia. They found that most of the good land near the coast had already been taken by English and Germans, so many Scots-Irish pushed on to the west and into Appalachia. That movement began a cultural and linguistic migration that continues to this day, as we shall see, gathering power and belated prestige in both North and South.

Until World War II, the accepted standard among the New York City elite was "r"-less. The speech of Franklin Delano Roosevelt, a New Yorker, illustrates the admired and widely imitated earlier style. FDR's speech was the model of an international English standard derived from the British Received Pronunciation that took its form in London, at the beginning of the nineteenth century. Not all Americans took to it, but the big Eastern "Tory" cities did. FDR had the prestige pattern of the upper class in New York. One can hear it in recorded excerpts from his Fireside Chats, such as this:

> To those who would not admit the possibility of the approach-
> ing storm,—the past two weeks have meant the shattering of
> many illusions—with this rude awakening has come fear, fear
> bordering on panic. I do not share these fears.

FDR did not pronounce "r"s after vowels, so that *storm* sounded like *stom* and *fear* like *feah*. William Labov points out that FDR also pronounced the "t"s in words such as *utter* and *shattering* in the British way, not blurring the "t"s almost into "d"s (*udder* and *shaddering*) as many of his countrymen did, and do. This British pattern was popular in movies of the 1920s and 1930s, when many American actors, especially if playing urbane or sophisticated roles, spoke with what some called a mid-Atlantic accent. And it was common on the radio, whose early broadcasters adopted that same standard. That held right up to the end of World War II.

People think that language evolves slowly over several generations, but sometimes it can change with dramatic abruptness. This was certainly the case with the once-prestigious "r"-less American accent.

"To our great astonishment," Labov told us, "it flipped. So, right after World War II, people growing up in New York City and in many other cities behaved in just the opposite way. When they were careful they pronounced their 'r's. And when they were not careful, were just speaking casually, they stayed with their 'r'-less dialect." In movies and radio soap operas, according to Labov, the "r"-less accent was abruptly confined to gangsters and comedians.

In 1966, Labov and colleagues began studying the changing role of "r" in the social stratification of the city. They chose New York department stores catering to customers they categorized as Lower and Working Class (Klein's), Lower Middle Class (Macy's), and Upper Middle Class (Saks Fifth Avenue). In each store the researchers asked questions to which they knew the answer was "fourth floor." The more fashionable or upmarket the store, the more the salespeople pronounced the "r"s in their replies, and the linguists assumed that the speech of the staffs resembled or mimicked that of their customers. Repeating the experiment in 1986 (with Mays replacing the defunct Klein's) and again in 1997, they found the use of the socially more acceptable "r" increasing about 1.5 percent a year. All the while, however, the "vernacular" speech of ordinary New Yorkers remained "r"-less. So—there is an evident, self-conscious class factor in how people wish their speech to be perceived. This is clear in the accents used on the popular series *Law and Order.* Lawyers, detectives in suits, and middle-class characters in general pronounce their "r"s. Uniformed policemen and policewomen and working-class characters do not.

Other researchers have noticed a similar pattern creeping into all of the traditionally "r"-less areas of the Eastern United States, Eastern New England, and the Upper and Lower South, meaning both inland and coastal areas of the South.

Linguist Walt Wolfram sees a lessening of the colonial linguistic mentality. "Let's face it, when I grew up—I mean, erudite people spoke British dialect, and there was no American dialect that was really anything but at best neutral."

It is ironic that many Americans who had found prestige in sounding more English began dropping it when admiration for Britain was at its absolute zenith, just after the joint Allied victory in World War II. Many Americans still harbor a twilight yearning for the sound of English speech. At about the same time as the first department-store study, there developed a vogue among New York businesses to hire British secretaries, whose accents were thought to lend a touch of class to Manhattan offices. When public television first emerged as a national force in the 1970s, some of its appeal lay in passionate viewer support for imported British series such as *Upstairs, Downstairs* and *Brideshead Revisited.* Considering the number of British imports and nature programs, Tom Shales, television critic for the *Washington Post,* observed that public television consisted largely of "English people talking and animals mating, occasionally interrupted by English people mating and animals talking." A young man in Greenwich, Connecticut, was asked whether his mother was English. "No," he said, laughing, "that's just a PBS accent."

Katharine Jones, a sociologist at Philadelphia University, herself a British immigrant, studied American attitudes toward English accents encountered by British expatriates living in the United States. She concluded that, in addition to being charmed by British accents, Americans often assumed British speakers were smarter and better educated and would always know what they were talking about. She quoted one Englishman as saying that if he wanted to get his point of view across he would emphasize the English accent, because others took more notice of him: "You suddenly become more eloquent. . . . It manipulates the situation. You can have people thinking that you are saying something more important than you actually are!"

In effect, while it lasted, this ascendancy of the "r"-less pronunciation amounted to a nascent American standard, and broadcasting helped provide a justification. What national broadcasters have always found desirable—although they have made exceptions—was an accent seemingly without accent, free of any features that gave it any particularly strong regional identity. And that is one definition of an American standard, perhaps the only one most Americans would buy.

In America's less hierarchical society, there has never been an official or socially imposed standard as there is in Britain, where the public schools (actually private, fee-paying schools) were set up in the nineteenth century to teach the sons of prosperous tradesmen to speak with a cultivated accent, like the sons of the aristocracy, who went to Eton. There they learned, as young people in England might say today, "to talk posh." What has emerged instead in the United States is a fairly stable grammatical standard with major variations in how it is spoken according to the different dialect regions. Thus the national standard is represented by broadcasters, but provincial standards are maintained in the speech of well-educated families in different parts of the country. One can hear this in the Congress—where Senator Trent Lott from Mississippi and Senator Edward Kennedy from Massachusetts both represent their regional standards.

Barbara Johnstone of Carnegie Mellon University puts a different spin on it: people from different parts of the country need to share a language, so that discussions about it "have to do with such things as clarity and correctness rather than with such things as friendliness and local pride." She teaches a course entitled "The Grammar of Standard Written English," even though she believes that there is no such thing as standard written English, that standards are a moving target.

When the issue is viewed another way, as with the effort to find an accent without regional identifiers, most linguists see a bottom-line standard in written American English as the absence of certain grammatical constructions, or "nonstandard" forms such as *ain't*, double negatives, and subject-verb disagreement.

Given all the regional diversity, and the great latitude in spoken language, what is fascinating is how passionately Americans care about being correct, with strong prejudices about "incorrect" regional features.

As a young man, Robert MacNeil experienced this at first hand. In his early twenties he wanted to be an actor, and spent the summer of 1952 at the Priscilla Beach Theater, one of the oldest barn theaters in New England. Half a century later, we found the theater still precariously in business, and actor-manager Geronimo Sands rehearsing a one-man show. The musty old barn, just reopened for the summer season, brought back vivid memories of the first time MacNeil stepped on this stage. Until then he'd been unaware that, with his Nova Scotia accent, he was pronouncing *out* and *about* to rhyme with *oat* or *boat*. The director said, "You can't talk like that if you want to be in this business." So MacNeil consciously began trying to modify those vowels, but found that it is not easy to change one's speech pattern—Shaw's Eliza Doolittle notwithstanding. To this day, he easily reverts to the sounds he learned as a child, especially when tired or back with his family in Nova Scotia, where the dialect, one of the family of North American Englishes, remains as strong as ever. The moral of this story is that, though Americans consider themselves egalitarian and unsnobbish, they are full of notions, often snobbish, about how *not* to speak.

We hold strong opinions about accents different from our own, and linguist Dennis Preston, of Michigan State University, has made those opinions his special study. Preston joined us on our way west by train from Philadelphia, as we headed into the Midland dialect region, which lies between the Northern and Southern regions. It is free enough of defining features of North and South to be considered, in Labov's phrase, the "default system of North American English."

Midland speech grew out of patterns that began in Philadelphia and migrated west through most of Pennsylvania, most of Ohio, Indiana, Illinois, and a large swath of America, including Missouri, Nebraska, Kansas, and northern Oklahoma, and then stretched away still farther to the west.

This speech pattern pronounces the "r" before and after vowels, and the word *rather* (as in *Dan Rather*) rhymes with *gather*—not with *father*, as in Boston. It avoids what linguists call the intrusive "r," pronouncing *saw* as *sawr* or, as John Kennedy did, *Cuba* as *Cuber*. It also avoids the Southern tendency to make *I* sound like *Ah*. Thus the Midland dialect is free of regional features of the South and the East Coast, which is why it was adopted as the standard for broadcasters once the prestige of the more British "r"-less speech had faded. Broadcast or network pronunciation is what most people take to be standard American.

When Bob Dole of Kansas ran for president in 1996, his Midland dialect sounded authentic to a lot of Americans. Of course, that year Bill Clinton's Arkansas accent had its own persuasive authenticity.

Some believe that Midland speech acquired its prestige as a reaction to two factors: the large increase in European immigration early in the twentieth century, just as the hitherto limitless abundance of free land in the West came to an end. This reality, often described as the "closing" of the Western frontier, had a huge psychological impact just when Eastern cities were filling up with immigrants from Southern and Eastern Europe, many of them Catholics and Jews. Many authorities claimed that the nation could no longer assimilate immigrants in such numbers as in the past. The anxiety was fed by xenophobia and anti-Semitism and culminated in the laws sharply reducing immigration after World War I. Harvard University became alarmed at the rising number of Jewish admissions (6 percent in 1908, but 22 percent by 1922) and moved to limit it. In 1922, a faculty committee was appointed to study a "more effective way of sifting of candidates for admission" and recommended building up "a new group of men from the West and South." This committee was headed by Charles H. Grandagent, a philologist with strong views on correct pronunciation, particularly the value of "r" after vowels. In his account of this process, Thomas Paul Bonfiglio says that Harvard thus "constructed the Nordic, Christian (mid)western country boy as the savior of its heritage," and the choice influenced other universities.

In this atmosphere, a wave of nostalgia for the purity of the West and frontier values swept popular culture. Out of it grew the sentimental and nostalgic figure of the cowboy as an American icon and then, as radio became popular, Will Rogers, "the plainspeaking plainsman with the heartland accent: male, Anglo-Saxon, individualist" and trustworthy. He was succeeded in the mid-thirties by John Wayne, as the Western folk hero. As the critic Eric Bentley wrote, "He speaks American. He walks American." Two other popular male movies stars of the period, Humphrey Bogart and James Cagney, both spoke like New Yorkers. By the end of the 1930s, Bonfiglio says, "New York speech had become dissonant with the notions of heartland American linguistic and ethnic purity."

This acceptance of Midwestern speech fits exactly with the results of Dennis Preston's research into prejudices Americans hold today about speech different from their own.

On the train taking us into the Midland area, Preston demonstrated the research technique he has been using for more than twenty years. He greeted strangers on the train, quickly established a rapport, and showed them a blank map of the country with only the state lines indicated. Hoping to reveal their "mental map" of American dialects, he asked his subjects to draw the areas where they thought people spoke differently. They seemed eager to do it, but immediately began identifying areas where they thought the least correct or the most correct English was spoken and drew circles around them. Preston said that nine times out of ten people will choose as bad or unacceptable English two areas, the South and New York City.

Referring to New York, a woman from Pennsylvania on the train told Preston contemptuously, "They say *waader*!"

"What do you say?" Preston asked.

"Water!" she said, firmly, with one word consigning New Yorkers to some cultural Lower Slobovia.

But as Preston also found among these train passengers, Americans are ambivalent about all of this. They may think New York and Southern accents are bad English, but they can also find these speech patterns charming.

One man told him, "I like hearing people from the South. I just like to hear the way they talk."

On one thing Preston's subjects almost universally agreed: the area we were traveling through was the zone of "normal English." Even Southerners "will reach right up and draw that Midwestern area and say it's normal." Preston added, "Many Southerners rate their own English as very, very poor, or least middling or not so good. And they've got some other part of the country, very often the Midwest, where they think people speak better."

The idea of what is correct or incorrect is fascinating because Americans seem to hold conflicting views. Preston believes that "there is a kind of lingering American insecurity that, well, maybe with English we don't do the very best thing. After all, we didn't invent English. It's really the English who had a hold of it before us. On the other hand, there's American populism and a desire not to be stuffy, not to be too correct—they detest too much correctness."

However, Preston said, "We still invest a lot of psychic energy, or whatever you want to call it, in paying a great deal of respect, a kind of unnecessary respect, to language correctness . . . so that bad language is associated with bad character. We say, for example, that somebody speaks dumb. Well, you can say dumb things in the most prestigious, well-educated dialect, and you can say really clever things in the most nonstandard variety. The associations are out of kilter."

Linguist Dennis Baron, who heads the English Department at the University of Illinois at Urbana-Champaign, says that, like it or not, people are always going to stereotype people by their speech. A friend of his once said of someone from the South that his speech "was so slow it was like bubbles coming up through a swamp. I guess that must be the way his mind works." Leaps like that are totally unwarranted, but they are made.

Barbara Johnstone says, "I think you just can't overdo the message that it's not the differences in language that are either correct or incorrect, or better or worse, or more familiar or comfortable, or whatever. It's differences in how people evaluate speakers of languages."

For Americans, standard, like politics, is local. Linguist John Fought says that if you went to Atlanta, for example, and tried to set up a practice that involves face-to-face interactions with people, you'd be at a disadvantage if you didn't have the right regional usage: "There's a standard, a social expectation that is defined for each group of people, in computer science or brain surgery."

* * *

Language is a growing thing, like a perennial garden, always throwing off new shoots, sometimes even new hybrids, needing constant thinning and pruning to preserve its vitality and beauty. In Shakespeare's unweeded garden, "things rank and gross in nature possess it merely."

Some purists see language change as producing things rank and gross and demand the strictest husbandry, while others welcome the vigor of new growth. With so many different ideas of what is correct or not, tolerable or intolerable, so much regional latitude, so much new growth, new expressions popping out all the time, so many social changes pressing on it, how is the language preserved at all?

William Labov casts a resigned eye on the process:

> Many older citizens . . . expend a great deal of effort in demonstrating to their children the illogical character of *aren't I,* or *like* as a conjunction. But even the most eloquent journalists and educators find that their rhetorical tools are not keen enough to cut the link that ties these forms to the younger speakers of the language. These defective forms return again and again until they are firmly fixed in the fabric of the language—when suddenly they appear as very natural and not at all defective, to all except a small group of traditionalists in professional and editorial chairs.

Thousands of Americans do not take so passive and tolerant a view. Out in the country are alert and zealous guardians of the language, like the armed camps the Romans maintained on the outer marches of the empire to guard civilization from the barbarian hordes. Perhaps that is an unfortunate analogy, since the barbarians eventually overran the Romans, and Latin, the language of empire, evolved into the many separate Romance languages. Though American English is unlikely to splinter into different regional languages, many dedicated Americans struggle to prevent further slippage into "defective forms," and to preserve what they see as correct standards in the written language.

One of them is Ulle Lewes, of Ohio Wesleyan University in Delaware, Ohio. A native of Estonia, she came to the United States having learned English after Estonian and German. English is her favorite. "Think about German," she says. "It does not borrow words, it does not invent new ones. That's one of the things I love about English. It is always getting new words from everywhere." As a person who takes such delight in the dynamic nature of English, Dr. Lewes seemed a surprisingly nonprescriptive person to head the Grammar Police, but that's what she calls herself. Twenty-five years ago, she took over the university's Writing Resource Center, and soon set up a hotline to answer calls about correct grammatical usage. To her surprise, calls started flooding in, especially after her group was written up in an airline magazine—calls from all over the country, including the White House, although the caller wouldn't say whose office. Today, there are grammar hotlines all over the United States and Canada, and each year they publish a directory.

Dr. Lewes told us, "A lot of people can't tell the difference between a gerund and a gerundive." That included us. Looking it up, we found that Fowler's *Modern English Usage* says the word *gerundive* has "no proper function in English grammar," but the *Random House Unabridged Dictionary* finds one: a *gerund* is a noun derived from a verb form—for instance, *walking*, as in *walking is good for you*. A *gerundive* has a form similar to the *gerund* but implies the necessity, obligation, or worthiness of the action to be done, as in *the book is worth reading*.

Dr. Lewes believes that her mission is to preserve the *grapholect*, the way we write, as opposed to *dialect*, which is the way we speak: "There are about sixty dialects of English on our planet—Pakistan, Nigeria, you name it. If you think about it, a person from Scotland with a brogue might not be able to communicate with a person from Texas with a drawl, or with a person from Nigeria with that very clipped speech. But if we all keep to the same grapholect, written rules, then we can still communicate."

To people who call the hotline to complain how the language is deteriorating, Ulle Lewes gives no easy comfort: "It's not deteriorating, it's just changing, so even the rules change. And when people call up wanting to know if something's right or wrong, we have to explain to them that Fowler says sixty percent of the experts think this way about it and forty percent think that way. Oh, that doesn't make them happy. They want a fixed rule, so we have to explain that some things don't have fixed rules."

Since rules are not fixed and continually evolve, with spoken usages creeping into written language, some linguists question whether the written standards *can* guarantee universal understanding, and tend to dismiss the efforts of hotline grammarians for delivering too reassuring a notion of correctness. But that's an academic issue in the practical world of newspapers. American newspapers print millions of words of copy every day, and each of those words will or should have been vetted by a copy editor. One of Ohio's leading papers is the *Columbus Dispatch*, whose offices are located across the street from the state capitol and one of the most eloquent war memorials in the country. The memorial consists only of words etched into stone panels, from letters written by Ohioans serving in the country's wars. The power of those simple, colloquial words is enormous.

Kirk Arnott, assistant managing editor, is the language cop or watchdog of the *Dispatch*. He believes in informal and conversational language, and that his paper should be as conversational as possible, to be accessible and clear to readers. He doesn't want it to "sound like the paper was edited by a schoolmarm. But somebody's got to keep the language from sliding into the abyss. Without policing it will tend to slide away from being a useful communication tool." He believes newspapers have a large role in maintaining the standards of the language, because people get used to what they see, and if they see it wrong they start repeating those misuses.

He also thinks that not just knowing what they're talking about but knowing how to say it goes to the heart of the newspaper's credibility. "I think if we use poor grammar or use words incorrectly people don't put a lot of stock in what they read." It is harder today, because the young people coming to work at the paper are not as well prepared as they ought to be; they're not getting the fundamental language training in school and college. "When I was in junior high school, I was taught to diagram sentences, and it did wonders for my understanding of how the language worked, and I don't think there are many teachers who do that anymore."

He's bothered by the misuse of words such as *importantly.* "All they mean to say is *important. Importantly* of course means to act as though you're important. *Bemused* is another one. People seem to think it means *amused,* rather than bewildered or preoccupied." Arnott mentioned *nonplussed,* meaning confused, but now used by some Americans to mean unperturbed.

Another factor is twenty-four-hour news on cable TV and radio, where much of the reporting is done ad lib, making acceptable the values of spoken language, discursive and colloquial, an intellectual exercise different from that demanded in written reportage. All his reporters and editors watch twenty-four-hour cable news, and "it just works its way into their heads."

Arnott's observation that not many teachers teach grammar nowadays is controversial but widely believed. Though teachers are obviously the first line of defense against language decay, many feel that society has stacked the deck against them. Linguist John Fought says that the consequences of not paying attention to your English teacher in America are much less than they might be in other countries, because the culture at large has a more relaxed attitude about these things. He believes that "it's a losing battle for the English teachers in the long run."

The National Council of Teachers of English issued a statement saying it was okay to split infinitives. "Well, that's a relief," said Fought, expressing the view of many professional linguists that holding the line on such rules as those against split infinitives, or insisting on *It is I* instead of the widely used *It's me,* is futile.

Geoffrey Nunberg, the Stanford linguist, said in one of his NPR commentaries that people writing software programs for computer spell-checkers "seem to pander more and more to all the infantile schoolroom prejudices that people have about usage." He quoted a woman who was developing such a program, who had been criticized by the salespeople for not flagging split infinitives. She said that was just a stupid superstition, and they said other spell-checkers had it and were using it as a selling point against hers. "So of course," Nunberg said, "in went the split infinitive along with all the other schoolroom fetishes that have been giving grammar a bad name for centuries—don't end a sentence with a preposition, don't begin a sentence with *and* or *but,* and of course avoid the passive."

To legions of Americans these are not stupid superstitions or fetishes at all, but rules close to holy writ. These people constitute a national guard, a ready militia of language watchdogs who believe that English teachers are shirking their duty and that newspapers don't set their language standards nearly high enough. Some are militant with good humor, others boiling with rage and scorn. Hundreds of them are members of SPELL, Society for the Preservation of English Language and Literature, with headquarters in Braselton, Georgia. In its handbook for members, SPELL's president, Jim Wallace, writes that the language is widely misused today by professional writers and commentators, as well as by the general public. "Perhaps worse, it is under attack by some teachers and grammarians who advocate permissiveness far beyond the normal processes by which the language evolves."

SPELL says it is not against change but change should not occur too fast, and therefore should be resisted. They quote John Ciardi's introduction to the *Harper Dictionary of Contemporary Usage:* "It will not do to resist uncompromisingly. Yet those who care have a duty to resist. Changes that occur against such resistance are tested changes. The language is better for them—and for the resistance."

SPELL members are encouraged to resist and to correct errors by sending Goof Cards, their "primary weapon," to newspapers or others they see abusing the language. We visited one SPELL member, Howard Vail, who regularly sends Goof Cards to newspapers and broadcasters from his home in Washington Court House, Ohio. A retired navy man in his seventies, Vail calls himself "the nitpicker" and will correct even a bowling buddy who says the ball *should have went.* He heard a baseball announcer say, *If he had went the other way, he would have caught the ball.* "People hear that and they use it. *Gone* has gone by, has *went* by the wayside," he says with a laugh. He found the sentence *Now it's up to you and I to convince them* in a letter from an organization wanting to have English made the official language of the United States. "Obviously it should be *between you and me.*" Vail has had a number of the goofs he's spotted printed in the society's regular publication, *SPELL/Binder.* He pointed to some other examples:

Her and some friend were getting ready to take advantage of the pleasant afternoon weather.

We lied in adjoining beds waiting for the doctors to take one of my kidneys.

Many of the errors they find are not grammatical but lapses in common sense in constructing sentences, such as one heard on a radio station in the early 1990s: *France is considering a TV campaign for condoms that will last until 1992.* "Kind of dangerous, I think," says Vail.

He tutors students for GED exams and is concerned about language instruction in schools. "Either they don't teach it or the kids don't pay any attention to it."

The National Commission on Writing in America's Schools and Colleges reported in 2003 that most fourth graders spent less than three hours a week writing, about 15 percent of the time they spent watching television. The panel of eighteen educators organized by the College Board said that if students are to learn, they must write. They found that only about half the nation's twelfth graders reported that they got regular assignments to write papers of three or more pages. The panel said that part of the problem was that in many high schools, with 120 to 200 students per class, just to read and grade even a single one-page paper per student would be a big task for a teacher. The report urged a five-year campaign to double the time students spend on writing, to get writing taught in all subjects, and to get each school district to set up a writing plan.

It is interesting that SPELL feels a need to protect literature as well as language, because American literature appears to be quite healthy today. American publishers boast long lists of living writers with international reputations, such as Kurt Vonnegut, John Updike, Philip Roth, Saul Bellow, Norman Mailer, Gore Vidal, Joan Didion, Susan Sontag, E. L. Doctorow, and Pat Conroy—to name a few. Their works and those of dozens of poets, nonfiction writers, playwrights, essayists, and critics carry out to the English-speaking world a linguistic standard of the highest order. And they are among the most admired examples of America's vast market in cultural exports. Americans truly worried about the state of the language have only to open one of their books, or the literary periodicals that discuss them, to see fine American prose, resting on a grammatical foundation that should reassure even the most exacting readers. It just doesn't get mentioned often in the debates about language.

Moreover, schools of writing have never been more popular. Indeed, Connie Eble, a professor of English at the University of North Carolina, Chapel Hill, says flatly that never in our history have so many people seriously undertaken the challenge to write or speak well. Editor of the influential journal *American Speech*, Dr. Eble says that at Chapel

Hill, as at universities across the country, they can fill as many creative writing sections as they can offer. "Many, many Americans still love the language of fine literature, and more and more people are interested in making it as well as reading it and hearing it. Carefully wrought American English is part of our national linguistic life, too."

But linguist John Fought says there is a "flattening of the hierarchy" even in publishing, a lot less layering of proofreading and copy editing and fact-checking, because the process is too expensive. "So standard writing is becoming more like speech, except in a few niches."

The encroachment of spoken language on the written has worried the writer Gore Vidal for decades. In 1984, he wrote: "As human society abandoned the oral tradition for the written text, the written culture is now being replaced by the audiovisual one. . . . What is to become of that written language which was for two millennia wisdom's only mold?"

Some would argue that computers, word processors, and e-mail are stimulating writing and bringing our generation back to the written word—at least until computers begin to understand spoken language. But that is the subject of a later chapter.

four

This Ain't Your Mama's South Anymore

The Ohio River has always been the traditional border between Southern and Northern speech, and we began our journey to the South down the Ohio on the *Belle of Cincinnati,* a reproduction riverboat deadheading from Cincinnati to the annual riverboat races in Louisville, Kentucky.

Although it carries heavy barge traffic of coal, cement, and sand, the Ohio is a bucolic river, running between lush, wooded banks—Kentucky to our left in the South, and Indiana on our right in the North. Much of it is so undeveloped that a traveler today can imagine how it looked to the first white settlers in the eighteenth century. Both the older maps of the *Dictionary of American Regional English,* based largely on eighteenth- and nineteenth-century word use, and the very new *Atlas of North American English,* created from current pronunciations, present the Ohio River as a linguistic frontier.

For many generations, Northerners have looked down their noses at Southern speech, but today many would be surprised to learn that the South has become the largest dialect area in the United States. More Americans now "speak Southern" than speak any other regional dialect.

The people who settled on the northern side, in Indiana, migrated down the Ohio—the biggest eastern tributary of the Mississippi. The southern side, in Kentucky, was settled primarily by Scots-Irish, who came overland through the Appalachians. In days when few people crossed the big river, most people on the northern side would say *I* almost as two syllables, like *Eye-ee*, whereas on the southern side Kentuckians would use the characteristically Southern monosyllable *Ah*. But with modern bridges and roads the two sounds have migrated back and forth across the river, in what linguists call a *bleedover effect*, and the two dialects merge a little. On the Indiana side are people who will say things that were classically identified as quite Southern. On the Kentucky side today you no longer hear the keen Appalachian dialect, which has retreated up into the hills. And even there it is disappearing. Where it does still survive, the word *there* becomes *thar*, *bear* is pronounced *barr*, and *hair* sounds like *herr;* and you might still hear expressions like *afeared, damnedest,* and *plumb right.*

Linguist Walt Wolfram, an expert on dialects, was traveling with us. On a laptop computer we played for him a scene from *The Story of English*, in which we drove up a long dirt road in the mountains to visit the weathered clapboard house of Ray Hicks and his wife, Rosa. This is how Mrs. Hicks told us to find their place:

> You fly in an aeroplane as far as you can come. Then you get in a car or a truck and ride as far as you can go in hit. Then you get down and run as far as you can. Then you crawl on your hands and knees as far as you can come. Go thataway and then you straighten up and then you find a house. It's a old-timey one. It looks haunted but it's really not.

Rosa's husband, Ray, was a well-known storyteller. We filmed him telling a Jack tale, one of a family of stories that includes "Jack and the Beanstalk." In this story, Ray tells how Jack meets a beggar who gives him a magic sack.

"He says, 'I'ma gonna give you somethin'.' He says, 'Here's a sack, that if anythin' gits to botherin' you, jus say, Wickedy-wack, into the sack.' "

Since we filmed them in the early 1980s, Ray and his wife have died, and with them two of the last authentic examples of the true Appalachian dialect. Walt Wolfram pointed out the traditional features—the *a-huntin'* and *a-fishin'*, saying *tar* for *tire*, adding an "h" so that *it* becomes *hit*. So the old mountain dialect, sometimes referred to as Hillbilly, has to be added to our list of disappearing dialects. But when we went ashore at a little place called Rabbit Hash, Kentucky, there were vigorous echoes of Appalachian speech in the vowels of an elderly fiddler, who talked of *over yander* and *a fur piece* and made *serve* sound like *sarve:* "And then when they treat a person you know, do a bad turn for 'em, instead of saying, 'I wouldn't serve a dog like that,' they'd say, 'I wouldn't *sarve a dawg* like that.' "

But if the Appalachian dialect in its purest, mountain usage is dying out, it is being reborn in a new and powerful way, because in its modern form it is absorbing other Southern dialects or accents and spreading itself across the Sun Belt—and farther.

You can hear its influence all over the United States in the lingo of truckers on their CB radios. We heard it while riding in the cab of an eighteen-wheeler with owner-driver David Swain. He normally talks with the Midland accent of his hometown, Hannibal, Missouri. But when he gets on the CB, where his nickname, or handle, is Spanky, he sounds "real country," although he can't say why: "I mean, my fiancée has told me. She goes, 'I just love to hear you talk on the CB,' and I'm like, 'What? I don't talk any different,' and she goes, 'Yeah, you do.' It's that CB slang, I guess. All over the country truckers pretty much sound the same way."

CB slang, like everything else, moves on. When we played some truckers' CB talk that we had recorded in the 1980s, Spanky didn't recognize many of the expressions, like *pedal to the metal*, meaning to drive fast, and *rawhiding a rig*, meaning to be rough on equipment. Now they say *get on up here* or *gas on it*. A weigh station, where trucks are assessed for state taxes, is called a *chicken house*, Spanky says, "because a lot of the drivers are chicken to go in there because of the logbook checking and the inspections."

CB slang has nicknames for cities. St. Louis is *Gateway,* Kansas City *Bright Lights,* and Nashville, where we were headed, is *Guitar* (pronounced *GIT-arr*), because "just about everybody up there's playin' guitars and singin'," Spanky says. "If you're gonna sing country music, you live in Guitar."

Country may be the greatest influence in spreading this dialect, known as Inland Southern. Spanky's nephew Cody James is a country singer-songwriter in Nashville, and we parked the rig to hear him perform one of his own songs:

> *Well, some things make me fightin' mad*
> *While I'm motorin' along.*
> *Like to watch a brand new backhoe*
> *Tear down a hundred year old barn.*
> *It makes me wish that I was rich*
> *Cause I'd buy up that farm land,*
> *Find the folks that were forced to sell*
> *And hand it back to them.*

Although Cody is also from Missouri, he sounds pure Nashville when he sings. Cody said, "When I fell in love with country music a long time ago, as a singer I started to emulate the singers that I liked. I think it's pretty simple. The more time that you spend in the South, you start to sound like the people that are around you. It's real comfortable and it's easier to talk that way than it is to start enunciating everything perfectly. It has character and it's friendly."

Music like Cody's—and the huge industry it fuels—is making *talkin' country* the casual, easygoing, informal way to speak American. You can hear it almost anywhere today, turning its Appalachian origins into a national trend. Linguist Dennis Preston says it used to be that, outside the South, "if you liked country music you were hopeless." But now if you like country music you can go downtown in the big cities in the North "and be a very hip person."

John Fought has studied the New South phenomenon—that vogue for Southern ways and country talk that now seems to reach farther and farther. For a long time, the most rapid population growth percentages in the United States have been in the Inland Southern area, the Sun Belt. And he says that trend is continuing: "This dialect has probably the largest body of speakers of any of the American dialects now. And this will only grow with time."

Working from census figures as well as linguistic data, Fought calculates that the Inland Southern dialect overtook Inland Northern in the past twenty years. By the year 2000, Southern speakers exceeded Northern by perhaps fifteen million. He includes big patches of southern Ohio, Indiana, and Illinois in the Inland Southern area below the Ohio River.

By contrast, the other strand of Southern speech, the "r"-less dialect of the coastal or plantation South, is losing influence. It is being swept away by time and advances in civil rights and the migration of Northerners, including millions of African Americans, who are moving south to enjoy the economic growth and warmer climate, a reversal of the twentieth-century migration to the North.

John Fought explains how these coastal areas came to be "r"-less in the first place. In parts of southeastern England, "r"-less pronunciation had become popular shortly before immigration to British North America effectively began with the arrival of the *Mayflower* in 1620. Most of the early colonists were from those parts of England. By 1750, the prime farmland of the Tidewater zone of the South was occupied by such settlers, who founded the system of plantation agriculture— large-scale capital-intensive farming, soon dominated by slave labor. They grew commerical crops such as rice, indigo, tobacco, and later cotton, most of which required a lot of water for cultivation and transportation. As they prospered, the proprietors of these plantations gave the "r"-less speech a prestige and social cachet, often reinforced by the sons they sent to schools in England. That prestige lasted well into modern times among those who cherished the tradition. The "r"-less feature did not penetrate to the inland South, because plantation farming was not feasible as the land grew hillier, and rivers had rapids or waterfalls, which made shipping of bulk cargoes impossible. It was into these mountainous areas of the South that the Scots-Irish came, because the easily worked coastal land had been taken. As we've seen, the Scots-Irish brought "r"-full speech with them, and nearly three centuries later, it is their speech that survives. The plantation system has long gone; the society it fostered has withered away, even in cities that once displayed its graces, such as Charleston, South Carolina. Their "r"-less speech is dying, with one paradoxical exception: it lives on the tongues of African Americans, whose speech was shaped in that coastal slave culture.

Today, it is becoming common for city dwellers in the Deep South to pronounce their "r"s. Labov says, "So all the young people you now interview in Mobile [Alabama] and Macon [Georgia] are pronouncing all their "r"s, not just in formal speech but everywhere. And one way of trying to understand that is that it's an expansion of a pattern that was always there in the Appalachian area, and the central South. And now it's moving out to the coastal area."

Having observed these changes since the civil-rights movement of the 1960s, John Fought believes that, as the population shift to the Sun Belt continues, "in time we should expect 'r'-full Southern to become accepted as standard American speech."

Linguist Crawford Feagin made a detailed study of accent change—and the disappearance of "r"-less speech—in her hometown, Anniston, Alabama, a small city in the foothills of the Appalachians. Located sixty miles east of Birmingham and ninety miles west of Atlanta, Anniston claims to be "in the very heart of the South." For a century it was dominated by iron-pipe manufacturing, until plastics changed that industry in the 1960s. Anniston is also home to a large U.S. Army weapons depot, where chemical and biological weapons were developed, leading to recent charges of massive air and water pollution.

Feagin found that upper-class people from Anniston were rapidly changing their characteristic "r"-less pronunciation. She traced it by recording three generations. A woman born in 1890 pronounced no "r"s after vowels in words like *her,* out of three hundred examples. A woman born in 1953 was pronouncing "r"s 64 percent of the time by the age of fifteen, and the grandson of the old lady had 93 percent "r"s.

Feagin's research told her that upper-class people were oriented away from Anniston, moving to cities like Birmingham and Atlanta and becoming less distinctively Southern. By contrast, those residents she termed working-class had stayed put and retained, even intensified, the "Southernness" in their speech.

Besides the adoption of the "r," there are changes in Southern vowels comparable to the Northern Cities Shift around the Great Lakes. Vowel changes in this Southern Shift include the shift of *shame* to *shime,* very similar to Australian and English Cockney; *age* to *aig; place* to *plice; same* to *sime.* These pronunciations were recorded in Birmingham, and may have had their beginning early in the twentieth century. The "oo" sound in *school* is changing, to produce *schuel.* Ghosts in the South no longer say *boo* but *bue,* a change Bill Labov sees spreading outside the South. So is the merging of the sounds in *pen* and *pin.*

In Cullman, Alabama, a smaller manufacturing town, we heard lots of talk about Northerners moving in. In the local coffee shop, the Busy Bee, we asked Kitty, one of the owners, what changes she had detected. "A lot of Northerners mainly is what I detect," she said. "You know, you can tell the Boston area, you can tell the New York area, just by their dialect. I think they come down here, they love it, and they stay. They do like to tease us about Southern accents, about saying *y'all.*" She was born in Puerto Rico but now says *y'all* herself. "Yes, I lived here long enough I picked it up."

Mike, the local barber, said he had customers from all over the United States, from as far away as California and Maine. One of his out-of-state customers said he just found himself sliding into talking Southern: "To say *y'all*, it's a relaxed form of communication and that's why people like it. It's fine, it's relaxing. You know, you see people on the news and they're speaking so properly and it seems so, I don't know, like work, I guess, when you're talking, as opposed to just relaxing and having a conversation."

The generational differences Crawford Feagin found in Anniston are the key to language change everywhere. Older people tend to speak as they grew up speaking, but their children and grandchildren sound different. That was evident when we moved over to Tunica, Mississippi, the flat cotton country bordering the great river, and famous as a cradle of the Blues. They used to work this land with mules; it took a hundred mule teams to work one local plantation. Mechanization arrived after World War II and drove people off the land. The blues and many black workers moved north, to be replaced in the 1990s by nine gambling casinos, attracting fifteen million players a year from all over the United States.

The small Methodist church in Robinsonville, a mile across the cotton fields from the casinos, has been reborn, welcoming gamblers and casino workers whatever faith they claim—Catholics, Baptists, Presbyterians—whoever turns up to join the locals who have been coming for generations. After the Sunday service, the church served a lunch of fried catfish outside, and we talked with some of the locals.

They consider their Delta Talk, as they call it, "pretty and gentler" than what they term Southern, but younger people's speech is changing. People in their thirties and forties are pronouncing their "r"s. One woman said, "We've moved to cities and stuff like that and come back, so you kind of integrate it, you know. The accents from the North come down here, and it all gets kind of integrated." A man told us, "I would say the young people don't have the drawl that the older people do. I think my Southern drawl is a lot more drawl than, say, these young people." His wife added, "And than our children. They speak more . . . a little better than I do. Not more proper but more understandable."

The casino presence makes Tunica quite atypical of most small towns in Mississippi. Its tax revenues have given the county a bonanza for roads and the highest per capita school expenditure in the state. But the local experience of Northerners pouring into this formerly closed rural society certainly dramatizes what is happening all over the South.

In the view of these churchgoers, it is also having something of a reverse effect, making Northerners less critical of Southern speech. These were some of the locals' comments:

"They seem to be charmed by it."

"If you go up north, they all want to gather round and listen to you talk, make no difference what you said."

"They love to listen to Southern."

Dennis Preston, the linguist who sampled Northern reactions on the train from Philadelphia, notes that a lot of historical things have happened, including the election of recent presidents from the South. Bigger cities, like Atlanta and Nashville, are no longer looked upon as outposts of American civilization. "People go there and they see stores, they see people dressed like they are in Chicago and Detroit. So the sort of Beverly Hillbillies caricature had faded, I think, just by acquaintance with what some people in fact refer to as a New South. So that New South is sort of escaping some of those caricatures of the Old South."

When John Kerry was competing in the 2004 presidential primaries, his Virginia campaign director, Susan Swecker, told reporters that the political complexion of the state had changed, and added, "This ain't your mama's South anymore."

The South has been hugely energized since it, for the most part, out-grew white resistance to black equality. It has become a powerful magnet for investment by America's big corporations and by such foreign coun-tries as Japan, Germany, and Britain. Southern states are among the fastest-growing in the country, transforming the region from an agrarian backwater to America's dynamic hub of transportation, banking, and manufacturing. Douglas Brinkley writes, "Downtowns which used to consist of one ugly skyscraper surrounded by 200,000 Baptists are now glitzy, multi-towered citadels, show-casing the buildings of such world-class architects as Philip Johnson, I. M. Pei, and Richard Meier." All of this helps to overcome Northern snobbishness about Southern speech.

Preston sees another amelioration of attitudes to the South based on a kind of romanticizing: "There's this popular urge among Americans: they don't want to sound stuffy. And when they don't want to sound stuffy they also want to sound friendly, pleasant, nice. And lots and lots of speakers very often identify the South as a pleasant place." Several Northerners he talked to on the train in Pennsylvania said it made them feel good to hear Southerners speak because it sounded friendly. "So that aspect of South-ern speech has done a lot to, not do away with the character—there's still very strong negative caricatures—but that's done away with it a bit."

To the extent that amelioration is happening, it's quite a contrast with the prejudice of two generations ago. Northern contempt for Southern values was as deeply rooted as the white racism that provoked the civil-rights movement of the 1960s. In Oxford, Mississippi, there were riots in 1962 when the first black student, James Meredith, was enrolled in the University of Mississippi. Whites in Oxford had bitter memories of the North, since the town was burned by Union forces in 1864. One of the antebellum houses that survived was the home of William Faulkner, the legendary writer. The bookstore on Oxford's main square is something of a shrine to Faulkner and another of the state's literary treasures, Eudora Welty. Welty lived in the state capital, Jackson, and had an accent different from the rather patrician speech of Faulkner.

She told a story about the impact of her accent in the late 1930s, when she attended Columbia University in New York. The woman who ran the women's residence would give free theater and concert tickets to the students. After a couple of months, Eudora went to her and asked, "Why did I never get any?" And the woman said, "With your accent we didn't think you'd be interested in cultural activities."

That kind of prejudice is still alive today, if somewhat better humored. In a recent film, *Sweet Home Alabama,* the character played by Josh Lucas, the good old boy who has stayed home while his wife, played by Reese Witherspoon, made a big career in New York, defends himself by saying, "Just because I talk slow doesn't mean I'm stupid." In the end, his glamorous, Northernized wife accepts that, as the audience is meant to.

In the 1950s, Lenny Bruce used do a stand-up act using a Southern accent while pretending to be Albert Einstein explaining relativity: "Y'all wanna hear about nooclear fishin?"

Today, the comedian Jeff Foxworthy builds his act around jokes about Southern speech, and audiences in the North and the South love it. Do Northern people think Southerners are stupid because of the way they talk? Foxworthy says, "Yes, I think so, and I think Southerners don't care that Northern people think that. In fact, I used to joke about that. I said nobody wants to hear their brain surgeon say, 'Right now, what we're gonna do is saw the top of your head off, root around in there with a stick, and see if we can find that dad-burned clot.' Nobody wants their brain surgeon talking like that."

Foxworthy fills the house and kills them with his "Southern" words:

"*May-o-naise.* Man, a's a lotta people here tonight."

"*Urinal.* I told my brother, '*You're in a l*ot a trouble when Daddy gets home.' "

"*Wichadidja.* Hey, you didn't bring your truck *with you, did you*?"

* * *

From Mississippi we headed into Louisiana. Our experience demonstrated once again that American speech is not being homogenized by media influence, but precisely the reverse.

The speech in New Orleans has origins as varied as the city's celebrated food, which Mark Twain called "as delicious as the less criminal forms of sin." In fact, New Orleans English has been called a *gumbo,* with ingredients from French, Spanish, Creole, later flavored by German, Irish, and Italian immigrants. But the ethnic group that gives Louisiana cooking and language added spice is the Cajuns. They are descendants of the Acadian French, who were expelled from Acadia, now Nova Scotia, when it became British and they wouldn't swear allegiance to the British crown. Their sad wanderings are dramatically rendered in Longfellow's poem *Evangeline.* Many Acadians found their way to Louisiana, still ruled by France until the Louisiana Purchase, and they settled mainly in rural areas. The town of Mamou (population three thousand) is in the heart of Cajun country, appropriately in Evangeline Parish, the Louisiana term for *county.*

To reach it, we drove by miles of cotton and rice fields, some flooded between rice seasons to cultivate freshwater crayfish, then made a turn by a tall water tower labeled "Mamou." Mamou has only one traffic light, but an international reputation as a headquarters for Cajun music. We stopped for coffee in Karl's restaurant, where several local characters were drinking coffee and gossiping alternately in French and Cajun English, a dialect that has emerged strongly in recent generations. To speak it is to be an insider in the Cajun community, given that the French language the older people speak is dying out.

In modern times, the 1921 Louisiana state constitution made English the official language, and schoolchildren were punished for speaking French. In Karl's restaurant, Blackie Fontenot said he couldn't speak a word of English when he began school in the 1940s but the teacher beat him every time she heard him speaking French or Cajun. "They spanked us, made us get on our knees," he said. "They were hard. Now they're trying to revive French. It's a shame what they did to us." Kenneth Courville, a Vietnam veteran, said, "Oh yeah! Dey do dat—pop, pop, pop, pop—ever' time dat dey hear de Cajun." Cajun English resembles some French Canadian English, with "d" making do for the "th" sound, which is difficult for most Francophones to pronounce. To these gentlemen, anyone from outside is an *American,* pronounced *Amer-ee-can.* Now their dialect has become, like *boudin* sausage, *crawfish pie,* and Cajun music, all bound together in a cultural package with big tourist appeal.

The chief attraction in town, right across the main drag from Karl's, is Fred's Lounge, where for more than half a century there has been a Cajun-music festival every Saturday morning. Visitors from many countries or from just down the road, some in leather biker gear, start arriving early for Bloody Marys while the four-piece band of drums, guitar, fiddle, and accordion warms up. By 9 a.m., people are packed in shoulder to shoulder, the drinks are flowing, and the tiny floor is rocking with people dancing the fast-paced Cajun two-step. Presiding over all of this is a mistress of ceremonies known as Tante Sue, a tiny dynamo of a woman who boasts seven great-grandchildren. She sings, cavorts, and sips hot schnapps from a half-pint holstered on her hip. She has an accordion printed on her T-shirt, and as she spins around, she grasps two strategically located points of material and, as she says, "I play my accordion on my T-shirt. I have a great time. I don't miss a note."

The whole bouncing, well-lubricated scene is broadcast live, with commercials in French and Cajun, on the local radio. The tempo of the music, the heat of the room, the hilarity of dancers and drinkers rise through the morning as everyone obeys the motto painted on the wall outside: *"Laissez les Bons Temps Rouler"* (Let the Good Times Roll). By 1:30 p.m., the session is over and people stagger out to spend the afternoon sleeping it off. Cajun culture seems alive and well—and lucrative—in Mamou, Louisiana.

Linguistically, Cajun includes expressions derived from French (*co faire* for *why?*; *dit mon la verité* for *tell me the truth*; *en colaire* for *to be angry*; *mo chagren* for *I'm sorry*), but it is nonetheless a dialect of English. It is just another way of speaking American—and speaking Southern.

* * *

It is not a long drive from Mamou to Texas. You can hardly miss the border: on one side of the highway is a towering Lone Star, three stories high. The speech of Texas, as big and as extroverted as that star, is another large swath of Inland Southern dialect, with its own variations and history.

Heading into the heart of Texas from Louisiana, we made a detour when we saw a sign for a place named Cut and Shoot. This is one of many names that show something extravagant and imaginative in the Texas personality. Others include Wink, Telephone, New Deal, Oatmeal, Old Glory, Pandora, Rainbow, Best, Bangs, Birthright, Cash, Deadwood, Grit, Gun Barrel City, Happy, and Joy. The population of Best, incidentally, is one.

Texas English is a combination of two Southern dialects. Some of those who settled came from the Lower South, plantation areas—Georgia, South Carolina, Alabama, Mississippi, and Louisiana—often bringing their slaves with them. Others came down from Appalachia, the Upper South—Tennessee, Kentucky, and North Carolina. To that mixture were added influences from Germans, Austrians, Poles, Italians, and Czechs who immigrated directly to Texas from Europe through the Gulf of Mexico. Since Texas was part of Mexico until 1836, Spanish was spoken here for a century before English, and a vivid Spanish influence survives in place-names and in the language of cattle ranching. The very word *ranch* came from the Spanish, as did *lariat, chaps, rodeo, bronco, poncho, pinto, stampede, corral, mustang, buckaroo,* and *vamoose*—the vocabulary burned into the American soul by countless cowboy movies. Whatever the legitimacy of this indelible national myth, some cowboys do exist, and we met a few on the Bar-J ranch, a spread of five thousand acres near Beeville, between San Antonio and Corpus Christi. And the pattern of their speech, slow-talking and laconic, suggested that Texas talk was naturally most at home on the range.

Jayk Linney, a part-time cowhand, described rounding up cattle for branding: "You just go at 'em kinda slow, and talk to 'em. You can't rush 'em, 'cos they'll go to tearin' down fences and all that. Like the cattle we worked earlier this mornin'. We went out there nice and slow, and they went straight for the brush. And they're probably still out there. It depends on how you work 'em and stuff."

This Texas talk is so seductive that outsiders who move here can't help picking up the twang. Linda Blackburn, who inherited the Bar-J from her late employer, originally came from New Mexico but now sounds pretty Texan as she describes what real cowboys are like: "Oh, well, I think number one is a real cowboy who's polite, mannerly to women, he has a kind of way with animals, including the dogs, the dogs are an important part of the team. And they're gentle, slow-movin', slow-talkin', just gentle people. Now, they'll fight if they're backed into a corner; then you've got a wildcat man, basically."

Since only 1 percent of Texans ride a horse to work nowadays, she sees a lot of wannabe cowboys, who are "loud, brawly, the big belt buckles, they have a lot of show. We call 'em drugstore cowboys, and they're the kind that are always in the fights, you know."

That tendency for newcomers to pick up features of Texas speech has been noted by Guy Bailey, provost of the University of Texas at San Antonio, and his wife, Jan Tillery, also a linguist, who have studied recent changes in Texas dialects. Texas has experienced the same population growth, particularly in the cities, as other parts of the South, and the nonnative arrivals are quick to pick up features such as *y'all* and *fixin' to*, just as some are to adopt big hats and belt buckles. Bailey says that in Texas, more than elsewhere, how you talk expresses your feelings about the state. "Those who think Texas is a good place to live, adopt the flat 'I' [*Ah*]—it's like the badge of Texas."

Parenthetically: a national survey conducted in 1996 found *y'all* spreading all over the United States. Outside the South, *y'all* or *you all* was used by 76 percent of Americans aged eighteen to twenty-four, even by 41 percent of those over sixty-five. That was halfway through Bill Clinton's presidency and before George W. Bush was elected.

Besides its own ways of pronouncing Southern English, Texas talk has another unique characteristic: it glories in wild metaphors and exaggerated similes, with a dash of braggadocio. We visited a collector of outlandish Texas expressions, Kinky Friedman, a most improbable Texan, his hair in long curled ringlets framing his face, calling himself both "Kinky the Friendly Cowboy" and "the only Jew in Texas who doesn't own real estate."

He got national attention with a music group called "Kinky Friedman and the Texas Jewboys," one of whose hits was entitled "They Don't Make Jews like Jesus Anymore." Since he left the music trade, Friedman has lived on a small farm in the Texas Hill Country near Bandera, where he churns out detective stories and other books, utilizing as much Texas idiom as he can stuff in. In his small study, employing the last typewriter in Texas (he thinks computers are the work of Satan), he displays pictures of himself with both Bill Clinton and George Bush, saying that he has now become a Friend of Presidents. Asked if he is President Bush's favorite author, Friedman says, "Yeah, but George is not that voracious a reader."

Though he was born in Chicago, Kinky has become a professional Texan, happy to share his store of Texas expressions: *Well, gutter my buff and call me a biscuit*, meaning *All right* or *Hi!*; *catty wompus*, for something that doesn't fit or is out of line; *dad blame it, dad bum it, dag nab it*, euphemisms to avoid swearing; *lurripin*, tastier than finger-lickin' good; *all swole up*, to mean *irritated* or *proud and self-absorbed*.

The place to hear Texas talk at its tallest is at the state capitol in Austin. The legislature is a kind of one-stop shopping for every kind of Texas accent. Although Texans are far from formal, this was the only place in our travels where we had to wear a jacket and tie. It was Celebrate Walker County Day, and one of the tributes read by the clerk recognized "Pancho Roberts and his wife, Sugar, as great Americans and great Texans" and concluded, "What a great time to live in Texas!"

Molly Ivins, columnist, author, commentator, and scourge of politicians, particularly male ones, joined us during a recess, to talk about Texas language. She told us: "We like our food spicy and we like our language spicy. This is one of the greatest places in Texas to hear it properly spoken. You get everything in this House of Representatives from the East Texas drawl to the West Texas twang. We've got guys serving in this House who sound exactly like Boom Hower on *King of the Hill*—you can barely understand a word they say, 'yo wng, wng.'" Molly sees Texas talk as having a "lunatic quality of exaggeration," and we asked what in the Texan psyche drives that. "I can't account for it, I can just tell it's there, this quality of being slightly larger than life in a pie-eyed way. I think the best explanation for Texas is, everything here is slightly exaggerated. And it leads to moments of great comedy."

One item on the legislative agenda that day was a bill to designate tortilla chips and salsa as the Official State Snack of Texas. "Now, that seems to me a noncontroversial resolution," Molly said. "We have always had a terrible time—we can't name a state dish, because the chili people, they're throwing food at the barbecue people, and you know there's just all kinds of bad feelings there. And then the Mexican-food people hop up, and what can you do?"

She also spoke of the wild metaphors characteristic of Texas speech. "Well, you get some wonderful expressions. Not original with me would be *meaner than a skillet full of rattlesnakes*. And then you get a whole bunch of them for *happy*. So—*if I was any happier, I'd just plumb drop my harp through this cloud*. Another one for *happy* is *I'm happy enough to be twins*. I have an old friend I camp with who always says, *I don't want to die and go to heaven 'cause it couldn't be better than this."*

But the real mark of eloquence is to invent your own: "The late Bob Bullock was a great speaker of Texan, and one day he was complaining about some young whippersnapper from the *Washington Post* who'd been in to interview him. To explain to me why he didn't like the guy, he said, 'Molly, his pants were so tight if he'd have farted it would have blowed his boots off.' "

Having a Texas accent gave Ivins some grief when she went to school in the East. "In fact, people generally subtract about fifty points from your IQ the minute they hear the accent. And I found it took me aback to find that people simply assumed that I was both a racist and an ignoramus just because of the way I talk. That was when I learned to speak without an accent, which I can still do when I concentrate."

One feature of Texas talk is how people employ it self-consciously as part of their identity. Linguist Barbara Johnstone, whom we met in Pittsburgh, studied the language of ten prominent Texas women, one of them Molly Ivins. She noted Ivins' ability to switch from earthy Texas talk to a highly literary standard English, and how this "style shifting" permitted Ivins to be both outsider and insider, as well as a liberal commentator in a conservative state. An example was Ivins' description of a 1970 debate in the legislature over the Clean Crapper Bill: "the delights of peein' against the back wall after a good whisky drank were limned with excruciating detail."

President Lyndon Johnson was a rich source of salty Texas expressions. He'd say about a dubious political ally, "I'd rather have him inside the tent pissin' out than outside the tent pissin' in." During the Vietnam War, when winning the "hearts and minds" of Vietnamese was the stated objective, Johnson would say, not so privately, "If I got 'em by the short 'n' curlies, the hearts and minds'll folla."

The LBJ Presidential Library in Austin has not totally surrendered to solemnity and has preserved some of the Johnson flavor for visitors.

An animatronic effigy waves its hands and rolls its eyes as it tells some of the folksy anecdotes Johnson would use to underline political points. One story goes like this:

> He reminds me of many great men I've known, particularly the schoolteacher that came out to apply for a job during the Depression in my little town of Johnson City. And the school board was divided on whether the world was round or flat and they asked him how he taught it and the poor fellow needed a job so much he said, "I can teach it either way!"

With LBJ, the uninhibited rhetoric and flamboyant style of Texas politics—plus the ability to teach it either way—hit Washington and brought to town regional dialects that the country wasn't used to hearing from presidents.

JFK's Massachusetts rasp grated on some and amazed others. His was the first presidential race that Molly Ivins was old enough to pay attention to. When her family sat down to watch the televised debate, "I could not believe that this man John Kennedy was not a comedian. I had never heard a Boston accent before. And he started talking about Cu-ber, Cu-ber, and I thought it must be a joke."

Kennedy's accent soon became part of his television charm, but LBJ's Texas speech was openly despised, especially by Kennedy people. Even by the late 1970s, Jimmy Carter's Georgia accent did him no favors in Washington. The country has come a long way since then. Former Rhodes scholar Bill Clinton saw no need to lose his Arkansas accent, partly because he could change it—or *code-switch,* as the linguists say—at will, depending on his audience. Then came President Bush, a scion of the East Coast establishment, ironically using a folksy Texas version of *talkin' country* as part of his political persona and winning in states far beyond the South.

Molly Ivins thinks the Texas/Southern influence is spreading: "I think the South has done rise again. There's a country-western song called 'Lubbock on Everything,' and sometimes I look at what's happening in the country and I think, Man, Texas on everything. I mean, I think the whole country is getting to be more like Texas, and frankly I think it's a terrible idea. Texas law and custom is kind of like Hungarian wine, it does not travel well."

Even as it travels, Texas speech is changing. Linguists Bailey and Tillery, with colleagues from Texas A & M and Oklahoma State University, have been "mapping" Texas speech by dividing the state into a grid with 116 squares. In each square they interview four people in four age groups. They have found the state divided into three areas: southeast, with the most Southern speech patterns; a middle strip running north to south, with a lot of variation; and a large swath to the west, with new speech features emerging. In the Dallas–Forth Worth metropolitan area, there are rapid changes. While newcomers adopt Texanisms, urban natives are abandoning some—for instance, dropping the *pen/pin* similarity, even as it's becoming more common in the rest of the country. Rural Texans may still say *tin cints*, but not urban Texans. City dwellers are dropping the "y" sound from *nyewspaper*, to say *noospaper*, and *toon* is replacing *tyewn*.

In West Texas, the researchers believe, a new dialect is emerging that combines features of Southern speech and another major dialect. In rural West Texas, they hear the vowels in words like *caught* and *cot* being merged, as are vowel pairs before "l" so that *pool* and *pull* sound alike, as do *feel* and *fill*, and *sale* and *sell*.

Even with these changes, the speech of Texas, like that of the rest of the South, is more proof that television is not driving Americans into speaking one uniform national dialect. Says Molly Ivins: "There was a popular intellectual theory about twenty years ago that the whole country was becoming more and more alike . . . but when I was a national reporter for the *New York Times*, what astonished me when I first went out there was the variety of humanity. And even the completely separate cultures that exist in the West—the Navajo backcountry, for example, where people not only don't speak English, they don't think like white people. You know, what's amazing is not the fragility of those cultures, it's their hardihood, it's their endurance. No, I really don't think that regional variations are gonna disappear. I'm amazed by the tenacity with which custom and dialect endure."

five

Hispanic Immigration: Reconquest or Assimilation?

The character of Texas owes a lot to its colorful history and to the wars with Mexico, through which not only Texas but New Mexico, Arizona, and California became American. That period of conquest (1829–48) was fired by the idea that it was America's Manifest Destiny to control the continent, and it increased U.S. territory by one-third. The legacy today is a two-thousand-mile border between two nations with the largest income gap of any adjoining countries in the world, with continuing tensions over migration and, for some Americans, over language.

When Spain ceded Florida by treaty in 1819, the United States renounced all claims to the Mexican province of Texas, but soon Americans began settling on the San Antonio River. In 1829, the United States tried to buy Texas, but the Mexicans refused. In December 1835, Texas declared itself independent; in February 1836, Mexico sent a large army under General Santa Anna to put down the rebellion. The Texas force, reduced to 187 men, retreated to an old Spanish mission in San Antonio called the Alamo. They scorned Santa Anna's call for surrender and, epically, resisted for twelve days until all were dead. In April, Santa Anna captured three hundred Texas soldiers and executed them all by firing squad. Enraged Texas forces under General Sam

Houston pursued and routed the Mexican army at San Jacinto. Santa Anna was forced to surrender all his forces and accept the independence of Texas. Sam Houston was elected president, and a struggle began for annexation by the United States, an idea resisted by antislavery forces in the U.S. Congress. Santa Anna, now president of Mexico, said that annexation would be an act of war. In 1845, President Polk tried to negotiate the annexation of Texas and to bargain for New Mexico and California. Again, no deal. The next year, U.S. troops moved to the Rio Grande, well inside what Mexico considered its border. Mexicans attacked, and President Polk declared war.

The antiwar protests that arose at home have a familiar ring in modern times. Whigs and abolitionists in the North claimed the war was contrived by Southerners to acquire another slave state. Former president John Quincy Adams denounced it as "a most unjust war." Henry David Thoreau spent a night in jail as a protest against having his taxes used to support the war.

After two years of fighting and thirteen thousand American deaths, U.S. marines entered Mexico City and added "the Halls of Montezuma" to the Marine Corps hymn. A minor State Department official, Nicholas Trist, negotiated the 1848 treaty of Guadalupe Hidalgo, in which Washington paid $15 million for most of what is now the Southwestern United States.

* * *

Ever since, the theme of *reconquista,* or reconquest, has surfaced periodically in romantic Mexican rhetoric. In 2001, the popular Mexican writer Elena Poniatowska declared that, thanks to immigration, Mexico is recovering the territories it lost to the United States in the nineteenth century. "The common people, the poor, the dirty, the lice-ridden, the cockroaches are advancing on the United States, a country that needs to speak Spanish because it has 33.5 million Hispanics who are imposing their culture," she said.

The idea of reconquest was deftly satirized by Jim Lehrer in the 1966 novel *Viva Max,* made into a film with Peter Ustinov, which imagined a bored Mexican general marching troops to San Antonio and retaking the Alamo. A delicious fuss ensues with much political huffing and posturing, all hilarious in the 1960s, when Mexican immigration was slight compared with today's numbers.

Today, talk of reconquest infuriates some Americans, who are worried about immigration and the Mexification of the Southwest: they hear more and more Spanish, and they fear that English is threatened. Others take a calmer view. The writer Richard Rodriguez says that Hispanic immigrants "are forcing us to see America within the Americas," and the result is that "Spanish is, unofficially, the second language of the United States, apparent on signs all over the city."

Rodriguez's city is San Francisco, but his observation is just as true in New York, whose subway riders might have been amused by the reference to cockroaches, *cucarachas,* as they read bilingual ads about how to fight the ultimate New York survivor with the Roach Motel. Its slogan: "Roaches check in, but they don't check out!" *Cucaracha* is old Mexican slang for poor and despised. "La Cucaracha" was a song created by followers of Mexican revolutionary Pancho Villa, ridiculing the government forces they said couldn't fight without smoking marijuana. Then it became one of the first popular Latin songs to break through into the American market. Recently La Cucaracha has emerged as the title and chief character, a human-size cockroach, of a satirical cartoon strip syndicated in more than sixty American newspapers. The comic *La Cucaracha* is shocking to many and draws plenty of hate mail because it ridicules Hispanic icons as readily as it mocks U.S. politics—evidence that the Latino presence in the United States has evolved to a level with many nuances.

Today, 27 percent of New York's population of eight million are Hispanic; in the Bronx it is 48 percent. At City Hall, of fifty-one council members, eleven are Latino. In Manhattan, when you take the Broadway subway uptown on weekday afternoons, the cars rapidly fill up with teenagers released from high schools on the West Side. Pale-skinned or very dark, most of them will be energetically speaking Spanish. If you take the crosstown bus on 125th Street traveling east, block by block you feel the English language disappearing as more and more liquor billboards and shop signs become Spanish.

We visited Spanish Harlem on a hot afternoon when rainy weather did nothing to dampen the fiesta spirit as Hispanics of many origins—Mexican, Latin and Central American, and Caribbean—got ready for the biggest annual Latino event, the Puerto Rican Day parade up Fifth Avenue. In New York, Puerto Ricans are the predominant and oldest of the Hispanic groups. Also, because of Puerto Rico's commonwealth status, one step below statehood, they are not quite immigrants in the way Mexicans are. In streets already festooned with Puerto Rican and a few Mexican flags, vendors were selling more flags and people were grabbing them to wave as they danced to the pulsing rhythms of *salsa* music blaring from shops and boom boxes. From the food stalls lining the streets wafted tantalizing odors of fried bananas, roast pig, octopus, and chicken with rice. Everywhere around us, the language spoken, sung, shouted, squawked over bullhorns was Spanish. It was as though we were not in an English-speaking country.

Large numbers of police officers in yellow rain slickers were on duty, because a Puerto Rican parade a few years before had ended in a riot when youths ran amok in Central Park, harassing and groping women. We asked the cops whether they could communicate with this large Hispanic population. Most of them said they spoke only a few words of Spanish but had no trouble being understood.

"Most people speak English. When there's a language barrier, I know a couple of Spanish words and manage to get by. But I haven't had a problem." That was said by a police captain whose father came from Chile and had never learned English. But the captain related this in an accent unmistakably from Brooklyn, where he grew up. So, in his case, the force of the city culture and schools had overridden his heritage. That has been the traditional immigrant pattern over the generations, when wave after wave of immigrants poured into New York as the gateway to the American Dream. Each tide has enriched American English with new words and expressions:

From the Dutch, who owned New York before the British bought Manhattan, came *blunderbuss, scow, sleigh, stoop, span, coleslaw, boss, bedspread, cookie, waffle, dunderhead, Santa Claus,* and *Yankee.*

From the millions of Irish immigrants came *smithereens, lollapalooza, speakeasy,* and *hooligan.* But the very American way of putting a definite article before institutions and conditions gave us *to the hospital,* whereas the British *go to hospital.* The president sends a message *to the Congress,* the British monarch sends one *to Parliament.*

Very few words came from the Scandinavian immigrants—*gravlax, smorgasbord*—but their speech heavily influenced the accents in Wisconsin and Minnesota.

Italians gave us names of food: *spaghetti, pasta, macaroni, ravioli, pizza, formaggio, mozzarella, lasagna, espresso, cannelloni, minestrone, Parmesan, broccoli, zucchini,* and *cappuccino.*

The linguistic imprint on American English of German and its Jewish relative, Yiddish, is on an altogether different scale. From German came *sauerkraut, pretzel, dumb, to loaf* and *loafer, ouch, bub, pumpernickel, kindergarten, nix, shyster, hoodlum, delicatessen, kaput, funk, hockshop, scram, bummer, check, cookbook, ecology, fresh, rifle, spiel,* and the suffix *-fest* on words like *song fest, foodfest, slug fest, talkfest.* German also gave us literal translations that became very popular in American English: *and how, no way, can be, will do.* Yiddish culture, which brought so much creativity to Hollywood and Tin Pan Alley, gave us *to kibbitz, schmaltz, schlock, nosh, phooey, schmo, schnozzle, to schlep, chutzpah, shiksa, bagel, pastrami, glitch,* and expressions such as *I should live so long, I should worry, Get lost, I'm coming already, I need it like I need a hole in the head.*

There were many German settlers in Pennsylvania before the Revolution, so many that there were early claims that the large numbers of German speakers threatened the primacy of English. Benjamin Franklin, whose print shop had published in German, wrote in 1751 that Pennsylvania "will in a few years become a German Colony: Instead of their learning our language, we must learn their's [sic], or live as in a foreign country." He also complained that Germans worked for lower wages, thereby taking jobs away from English workers—a note that would be sounded often over the centuries. But to win the Germans over, the Continental Congress printed German translations of some of its deliberations, including the Articles of Confederation, and German Americans did support the Revolution.

After 1776, seven million more Germans arrived, mostly to settle in cities such as Cleveland, Cincinnati, Milwaukee, Chicago, St. Louis, Buffalo, and New York, as well as Texas. Many of the Germans were educated, middle-class people who quickly made a cultural impact. There were twenty-eight German-language newspapers by 1860, and German achievements in music, literature, and science gave these immigrants a prominent and welcome place in American society—until World War I. At the turn of the century, one American in ten was speaking German, almost exactly the percentage who are currently speaking Spanish. In Texas the percentage was much higher, for the broad belt of German settlement ran from just west of Houston through San Antonio to Fredericksburg. Many of the most prominent American families were of German stock: the Astors, Budweisers, Eisenhowers, Fricks, Heinzes, Rockefellers, Singers, Steinways, and Westinghouses.

But when a German submarine torpedoed the Cunard liner *Lusitania* in May 1915, killing 1,195 of the 1,959 people on board, it outraged the American public and helped create the climate for Washington's declaration of war in 1917. The Germans became *Huns, Boche,* or *Jerry,* as Americans borrowed British and French epithets. In this atmosphere, many changed obviously German names—for example, *Stein* to *Stone.*

Frankfurters became *hot dogs,* and to some Americans *sauerkraut* became *liberty cabbage* (as our generation tried making *French fries* into *freedom fries* to punish France for not joining the 2003 invasion of Iraq).

In the new climate, one state after another banned German instruction from its schools. In 1918, when the New York City School Board did so, the *New York Times* applauded; dropping German was "a matter of polity, of patriotism, of Americanism." German was "suspect and taboo," a poignant judgment for a newspaper published by Adolph S. Ochs, who grew up in a German-speaking home.

Ironically, given today's linguistic anxieties, in the same editorial the *Times* suggested that, if a second language was needed at all, Spanish would be more useful for business. As the war fever spread, all foreign languages became suspect, and Washington made it illegal to mail non-English written matter if it mentioned the U.S. government or the war. The governor of Iowa banned the use of any foreign language in the schools, in public, or on the telephone.

Immediately after the war, a wave of Americanization swept the nation's schools, including a "Good English Makes Good Americans" campaign. Children earned points for snitching to teachers on the language errors of their classmates. These campaigns produced loyalty oaths such as the "Pledge for Children" of the Chicago Woman's Club American Speech Committee:

I love the United States of America. I love my country's flag. I love my country's language. I promise:

1. That I will not dishonor my country's speech by leaving off the last syllables of words.
2. That I will say a good American "yes" and "no" in place of an Indian grunt "um-hum" and "nup-um" or a foreign "ya," or "yeh" and "nope."

3. That I will do my best to improve American speech by avoiding loud, rough tones, by enunciating distinctly, and by speaking pleasantly, clearly, and sincerely.
4. That I will learn to articulate correctly as many words as possible during the year.

Although Congress cut off most immigration in 1924, this wave of linguistic discrimination, or paranoia, passed. By the 1930s, the federal government was explaining the New Deal in every language spoken in the country.

With immigration resumed after World War II, New York again became its doorway, and remains so to this day. In the 1990s, New York gained population but lost half a million white people; all of the gain in population came from minority-group immigrants. The ethnic complexion of New York neighborhoods continues to shift, like the nationalities of taxi drivers. In a Manhattan taxi, we met Dave Pollack, one of the few American-born cabbies, who grew up in the Bronx. His grandfather came from Russia and also drove a cab. "This is where you start," he said. "Actually, driving a cab is a great way to start earning money. But years ago it was the Irish, people from Italy, people from the Ukraine, many parts of Europe. Today the countries are Pakistan, India, and Bangladesh, but they're going through exactly what my grandfather did almost a hundred years ago."

An ad in the New York subway claims, "There are more than 250 languages spoken in New York City. How many should you speak?" The 2000 census showed large increases nationally from 1990 in many immigrant languages people said they spoke at home. The number of those who spoke Chinese, Vietnamese, Russian, and Arabic almost doubled, the largest group of these, Chinese speakers, growing from 1.2 million to two million. But far and away the non-English language most people said they spoke at home was Spanish, an increase from seventeen million to twenty-eight million in the same decade.

That statistic raises the question, Will the traditional pattern of assimilation by the second and third generations repeat itself with Spanish-speaking immigrants today, or are their concentrated numbers too large? By July 2002, the Census Bureau reported that all together there were 38.8 million Hispanics or Latinos (the bureau uses both terms) in the United States, 60 percent of them born here. The Hispanic population had doubled since 1980, because of a high birthrate and high levels of immigration, legal and illegal. Two-thirds were of Mexican origin. Given this growth rate, one in five residents of the United States is expected to be Hispanic by 2020.

There are large districts of major American cities—New York, Los Angeles, Miami—and many smaller cities where it is possible to live and never speak English. In Harlem, we talked to a woman named Rosa selling shaved ice flavored with syrup. She had lived in the United States for nineteen years but spoke no English. She explained that she was always too busy working to learn.

This ability to survive within an all-Spanish community has been enhanced by the growth of Spanish-language media. Between 1990 and 2002, the number of Spanish-language newspapers published in the United States grew from 355 to 652. Many are published by well-respected English-language papers—such as the *Miami Herald, Dallas Morning News, Los Angeles Times,* and *Wall Street Journal*—both to make up for the continuing loss of English-language circulation and to attract advertisers to the surging Hispanic market.

Gilbert Bailon, president and editor of the *Dallas Morning News,* said the Spanish-language *Al Día* was created to reach a growing number of people in the market who are primary Spanish speakers. "These people are neither reading nor consuming our advertising in the way we would like, and really need, for the future of this company to grow." He said there was a good editorial reason as well: "You can go on the web and read lots of papers around the world, but they can't tell you what the school lunch menu is, or are the roads closed, or when I can vote in Dallas, Texas, or San Antonio, Texas, because it's just not there in Spanish."

It is the same story in broadcasting. By 2002, there were 664 Hispanic radio stations and 252 TV stations served by twenty-six Spanish-language TV networks. The big network Univision claims to reach 98 percent of U.S. Hispanic households through its Spanish-language television network and 73 percent with its radio network. Its rival Telemundo, owned by General Electric and managed by NBC, is viewed in 118 markets and says it reaches 91 percent of Hispanic TV-owning households.

In surprising places like Raleigh, North Carolina (a state that saw a fivefold increase in Hispanic population in the 1990s), Spanish TV rivals and sometimes attracts larger audiences than the network outlets of NBC, CBS, and ABC. Interestingly, a new dialect has been emerging in North Carolina, where Hispanic migrants have mixed Spanish with Southern rural speech and created, in Walt Wolfram's terms, "an Hispanic Southern variety of English." Yet among the products frequently advertised on Univision television and Spanish-language radio are English-study kits on CDs or cassette tapes.

The 2000 census showed the states with the largest Hispanic immigrant concentrations (based on number of persons who speak Spanish at home) to be New Mexico with 29 percent; Texas, 27 percent; California, 26 percent; Arizona, 20 percent; Florida, 16 percent; Nevada, 16 percent; New York, 14 percent; New Jersey, 12 percent; and Illinois and Colorado, each 11 percent.

The city with the highest percentage of people speaking Spanish at home was Hialeah, Florida, with 92 percent. Number two, with 91 percent, was Laredo, Texas, right on the Mexican border, and we traveled there to understand the concerns and tensions the language situation provokes.

And it was there that we heard the word *reconquest*. Reconquest is real to Allan Wall, a language teacher we met who is married to a Mexican and lives in Mexico with his wife and children. Every morning it is rush hour on the international bridge across the Rio Grande from Neuvo Laredo. Traffic crawled so slowly our first morning that it was quicker for Wall to park his car and walk across to the United States. Wall is an American so alarmed by the spread of Spanish that he wants English made our official language. He offers the classic reasons: "It's a great advantage for us to have a common language. It's good for immigrants to learn English. It opens up to the mainstream of the American society and economy. It's also an important part of our common citizenship; the Declaration of Independence, the Constitution, the Bill of Rights, the judicial precedents, all these are in English." Wall sees tolerance for Spanish as a threat to the linguistic unity of America, to our common civic language, which could lead to a linguistic Balkanization of the United States.

In Laredo, Spanish is effectively the city's language. In the local supermarket, the loudspeaker announcements of specials are in Spanish. The local newspaper, the *Laredo Morning Times,* publishes editions in both Spanish and English. The city editor, Robert Garcia, noted that major newspapers across the United States were switching some of their sections to Spanish, "because they need to get to those folks, to communicate with those folks." He himself works with both language populations, "so I am constantly switching back and forth, you know, but I'm used to that: I'm from the area."

To see how the Spanish language had reasserted itself in the border area, we went to a small town southeast of Laredo, called El Cenizo, Texas. In Spanish, *el cenizo* means *the place where there are ashes,* which could suggest a town rising phoenixlike from a destructive past or a town still in mourning. In view of the extreme poverty and underdevelopment, and the rather depressed appearance of the town, the latter interpretation was not unkind. We had an appointment to see the mayor of El Cenizo but found she was in Laredo, at a meeting to secure funds to start a library. Town officials have set aside a small room in the cinder-block town hall, but it had no books when we visited.

In 1999, the previous mayor put El Cenizo on the map, and in the gun sights of English-firsters, by declaring Spanish the town's official language. The rationale was democratic, to make their town government more accessible to the nine hundred residents, few of whom spoke English, including the mayor himself. If residents understood the town business, they might be willing to pay their taxes, which conspicuously they were not, to pave local roads and improve facilities for their children. But El Cenizo found itself at the center of a national furor.

Newspaper editor Robert Garcia said, "It was ugly. They got calls, threats, people telling them, 'You're in America, what are you doing speaking Spanish as an official language?' " He showed us a pile of hostile editorials and stories from as far away as Boston and Florida, with the headlines "No Inglés!"; "Banning English Divisive Measure"; "Hot in Any Language"; "Town's Ordinance a Step Backwards"; "Small Town News Can Grow Big and Ugly"; "Texas Town Makes Spanish Official, Stirs War of Words." A lot of other nearby towns wanted to do the same, but after the reaction to El Cenizo they backed off.

El Cenizo compounded the affront by passing an ordinance that no town official (there were two at the time) had to collaborate with U.S. Immigration authorities or the Border Patrol. The next mayor of El Cenizo, Oralia Reyes, hastily reversed both policies.

El Cenizo's main street runs past shabby trailer homes planted in neglected lots down to the Rio Grande. Here the river border with Mexico is one of the most-traveled crossing points for illegal immigrants. The river is about a hundred yards wide at this point, the banks masked on both sides by trees and bushes. On the El Cenizo bank we found discarded inner tubes, used to float people across by night, along with the wet clothes they had abandoned and the black plastic bags that had carried the dry clothes they changed into. Because it is so frequently used, this area is heavily watched by the Border Patrol, and we spent a day seeing how they track *illegals,* the new official term, replacing *wetbacks,* the now derogatory name for Mexicans who swam the Rio Grande to reach the United States. But informally, among themselves, the agents say *wets,* as one did with us: "You want to chase wets? We'll chase wets."

The U.S. government estimates that there are eight million illegal immigrants in the country, of whom 70 percent probably came across the Mexican border. The Border Patrol has been given increased resources to reduce that flow, but readily admits that it cannot come close to stopping it.

The agency's effort in this area begins with electronic sensors (called *bugs*) installed near the riverbanks. Agents then patrol stretches of open bush country a few miles inland from the river. This includes the unpaved roads the illegals have to cross to move farther inland to rendezvous with trucks organized by their *coyotes*—the people who make a living smuggling Mexicans across the border and helping them escape into the U.S. interior. The places the illegals habitually cross are dragged each day, to erase old footprints. When the electronic sensors are tripped (or *the bugs go off,* as the agents say), indicating a fresh crossing at a certain point, the patrol drives along the dirt track searching for new footprints. They are easy to spot, unless the crossers used a branch to sweep the earth behind them, as some do, or sneaked through the occasional drainage culvert. When the agents see fresh footprints, they can follow the tracks on foot and radio for a helicopter to search ahead. They call it *sign cutting,* following tracks or *signs,* while the helicopter *cuts in* ahead. Sometimes the agents will put toilet paper on bushes so the helicopter can see where they have been. "You can't *cut* just one person," an agent says, meaning you need a group to make the tracks evident, and the *coyotes* usually bring the *IA* (illegal aliens) in groups, often sending scouts across first to reconnoiter the route. If alarmed, the *coyotes* will halt a group under bushes in a gully during the day, to move them on by night. It is not pleasant terrain. The sandy earth is thickly covered with brush—mesquite, some cactus, and bushes with sharp thorns, which easily tear clothes or flesh, especially in the dark. During certain seasons, there are snakes—black indigos, rattlesnakes, corals, and water moccasins. There are other dangers, including, in some border areas, border-zone vigilantes reportedly going out to shoot and kill illegals. Federal and state authorities have tried to find and stop such people, without success. In the desert areas farther west, many illegals die of thirst each year, because they run out of water before they can get across. The Border Patrol has taken to setting bottles of water along frequently used routes to prevent that.

Despite the dangers, the Mexicans keep coming. The Border Patrol agents we accompanied believe they get about 40 to 50 percent of the people who cross in this area, but overall the percentage is perhaps only 10 percent.

This unit caught a dozen immigrants late that afternoon. A woman agent spotted their tracks and alerted the helicopter, which buzzed in a few feet above the brush and found the Mexicans, crouched in a hollow in the shadow of the bushes. We could hear the helicopter pilot's excited voice on the radio: "Bodies! Bodies!" When the agent made the arrest, the Mexicans offered no resistance, and no one attempted to run away. A bus was sent in, and they were driven off to be fingerprinted and checked for any criminal records. If there was evidence that they were *coyotes* or *mules* (drug carriers), they would be arrested. Those who had simply come across the border would be delivered back to Mexico. They usually try again, and frequently, because the odds of getting away with it are good.

Allan Wall, the teacher, said that living in Mexico had given him a different perspective on the inroads of Spanish in America. He recalled a Congress of the Spanish Language in Madrid in 2001. One of the speakers was Vicente Fox, the president of Mexico, who commented that Mexican immigrants who continue to speak Spanish in the United States are doing their patriotic duty to Mexico. Another speaker was Carlos Fuentes, perhaps the leading literary figure in Mexico. "He said that there is a silent *reconquista,* a reconquest of the United States. He didn't even limit it to the Southwest, as many do; he just said 'of the United States.' "

To prevent this, Wall wants immigration reduced, to give legal immigrants time to assimilate. He not only wants English made the official U.S. language, but wants all government business to be in English. If people don't understand English, they will be motivated to learn, he believes, because some Hispanics are "impeded" from learning by U.S. government policies, such as the translation of documents, bilingual education, and bilingual election ballots. He sees American politicians pandering by speaking Spanish themselves to woo Hispanic voters— one of these George W. Bush. Wall faulted Bush, as governor of Texas, for not taking action, like cutting off state funds, after the El Cenizo ordinance. He also noted that Bush, as president, was on record as opposing the English Language Amendment.

The growing Latino presence has created tensions. In the Maryland and Virginia areas that are part of the Washington, D.C., metropolitan area, designated one of hypergrowth for Hispanics, there have been clashes over issuing drivers' licenses and offering the reduced in-state tuition rates to illegal immigrants. Steven Camarota, research director of the Center for Immigration Studies (which wants immigration limited), said the numbers raise a troubling question: "Is the level of immigration so high that it's overwhelming the assimilation process?"

Immigrant is a word coined in America, for migrants who came *in,* rather than went *out,* the meaning of *emigrant,* which was how Europe saw it. But despite living in a nation built on immigration, Americans already here have always had ambivalent feelings about those just arriving. In his study of the history of immigration and language, *The English-Only Question,* Dennis Baron wrote:

Settled Americans have been reluctant to accept newcomers, regarding them as socially, economically, and racially inferior, more insistent on special concessions like bilingual ballots, and on government handouts, and less willing to assimilate than earlier generations had been. These negative attitudes find their focus in attacks on minority languages, which are all too obviously badges of ethnicity.

Recently Hispanic immigration has raised new expressions of anxiety in that vein. Victor Davis Hanson, a fifth-generation Californian, argues that continuation of the status quo—with virtually open borders, and multiculturalism in the schools—would mean a general breakdown of the old assimilationist model. If so, we would end up with *Mexifornia*—he has written a book with this title—a "hybrid civilization," in which "Spanish has equal status with English and there is little Americanization."

Political scientist Samuel P. Huntington, chairman of the Harvard Academy for International and Area Studies, claims that "the single most immediate and most serious challenge to America's traditional identity comes from the immense and continuing immigration from Latin America, especially Mexico." In a book entitled *Who Are We?* Huntington says that Mexican immigration is unique and contradicts the tradition of assimilation. He summarized his argument in *Foreign Policy* magazine. Previous ethnic groups arrived in waves that began and ended, giving time for the immigrants to be assimilated, whereas the Mexican wave is continuous. Mexicans, he argues, do not assimilate and become truly American, because they do not embrace American values and ideals: they do not share the work ethic inherited from America's Anglo-Protestant culture; they do not have the same hunger for education; proportionately fewer go to college; fewer have incomes above $50,000 a year; fewer hold managerial positions. Moreover, he claims, "As their numbers increase, Mexican Americans feel increasingly comfortable with their own culture and often contemptuous of

American culture." Hispanic people, finding strength in numbers, create a growing Latin influence in entertainment, advertising, and politics. One index foretells the future: "In 1998, *José* replaced *Michael* as the most popular name for newborn boys in both California and Texas." Further, the Mexican fertility rate is higher than for other Americans, "a characteristic of developing countries."

This assault brought instant rebuttal. David Brooks, a columnist in the *New York Times,* wrote that the most persuasive evidence is against Huntington, because "Mexicans *are* assimilating." He quotes the book *Remaking the American Mainstream,* by Richard Alba of the State University of New York at Albany and Victor Nee of Cornell: "Although there are some border neighborhoods where immigrants are slow to learn English, Mexicans nationwide know they must learn it to get ahead. By the third generation, 60 percent of Mexican-American children speak *only* English at home." Objecting to Huntington's use of the term "Anglo-Protestant" to describe American culture, Brooks argues, "There are no significant differences between Mexican-American lifestyles and other American lifestyles. They serve in the military—and die for this nation—at comparable rates."

Anxieties/perils/visions like Huntington's are not new, but since 1981 they have been driving a national movement to make English the official language of the United States. It surprises many people to know that English has never had any constitutional privilege. The movement to change was supported by such prominent people as the late Alistair Cooke and Senator S. I. Hayakawa. Cooke wrote, "The day that the immigrant's tongue becomes the first language of any community or—God forbid—a state, the American experiment will be in serious jeopardy of falling apart." Hayakawa, the noted semantics professor who became a senator, introduced the English Language Amendment to the constitution in 1981 and helped found the organization U.S. English, to promote it nationally. He wrote, "In order for us to cooperate most fully with our families, friends, neighbors, co-workers, and fellow citizens, we must not only have a language; we must have a common language. If we do not, our future holds a terrifying potential for conflict." The movement sees efforts at bilingual education in schools and government concessions to non-English speakers, such as election ballots in foreign languages, as wrongheaded, because they slow the acquisition of English and hence assimilation.

For some there is also an immigration reform agenda. The U.S. English organization suffered a public-relations disaster in 1988, when Dr. John Tanton, another founder, advocated forced sterilization as a means of population and immigration control. Several noted supporters, including Walter Cronkite and Linda Chavez, an influential Hispanic Republican, resigned in protest.

The English Language Amendment to the U.S. Constitution, although frequently reintroduced, has gone nowhere. In 1988, Congress held one day of hearings. Dennis Baron wrote that the hearings reiterated the two arguments that have informed such discussions for two centuries: an insistence that English is the glue holding an ethnically diverse America together, and a fear that official-language legislation masks racial discrimination—in this case against Hispanic Americans. Claims that English is the key to an understanding of American ideals are balanced against warnings that voters will be disenfranchised and the public safety endangered by restrictions on government use of languages other than English.

There has been more action in the states, about half of which have enacted official-language laws, although the demand for such action has quieted down recently. In the late 1990s, Colorado, Florida, and Arizona passed laws, though only Arizona's had teeth: it said that no public official could communicate in any language other than English. But federal law administered by state officials often required translation into other languages. State employees, saying they had to obey federal law, sued and won. The law was overturned by a U.S. circuit court, and the U.S. Supreme Court refused to hear an appeal. Now the movement has descended to the municipal level, with a town here or there passing an English-only ordinance, which has little effect.

The impracticality of such laws is obvious, given the American economy's apparent need for millions of Hispanic immigrants. Though generations of educated Hispanics have advanced in all areas of American life, the recent arrivals from poor villages in Mexico do much of the menial work in this country. Predominantly in the Southwest, but all over the country, Latino men and women wash restaurant dishes, make motel beds, care for children, clean hospital rooms, mow lawns and trim hedges, and do small construction projects. They also cultivate and pick the fruit and vegetables that fill our supermarkets. They do these tasks for wages lower than non-Hispanic Americans will accept, often below minimum wage, and although it is illegal, they can be exploited by employers—blackmailed, in effect—for being undocumented aliens. The jobs they fill cannot be exported directly to the Third World, but these low-wage workers are imported from it, and the effect on the global economy is the same.

More recently, President Bush proposed granting legal status to some of the eight million workers in the country employed illegally, giving them renewable work visas. But eventually the illegals would have to return to Mexico, or wherever they came from. Democrats criticized that plan for not helping such immigrants move toward citizenship; some Republicans felt it did not do enough to slow down the flow of Mexicans across the border.

To what extent is the fear of reconquest justified?

Certainly, in one mundane part of our culture, Mexico has "conquered" a portion of the American food market. The *OED* recently noted the growing popularity of Mexican food by adding *huevos rancheros* (eggs on a *tortilla* with sausage, beans, and *salsa*). In the mid-1990s, a taste milestone was passed when sales of *salsa* exceeded those of ketchup. Food terms such as *taco, enchilada, chili, burrito, ceviche, empanada, guacamole, jalapeño,* and *tamale* are common in the American vocabulary from the proliferation of Tex-Mex and Mexican restaurants, and supermarkets as far away as New England offer large sections with Mexican ingredients. But that is broadening American tastes. Reconquest, taken literally in the linguistic sense, would mean the replacement of English by Spanish—*the whole enchilada,* so to speak. In cities like Laredo it might appear that this is happening, but there is contrary evidence. For example, Spanish appears to be losing ground in San Antonio, where the very old Hispanic population has now been in large part assimilated into the Anglo community.

* * *

To pursue this question, we traveled to California, another part of the former Spanish overseas empire, to explore the degree to which Spanish is "reconquering" the country's most populous state.

What is evident is that when Spanish and English rub against each other intimately they produce hybrids. Our first stop was a television station in Los Angeles, and a program called *Mex 2 the Max,* starring Patricia Lopez, a former fashion model, who has a new career as a *VJ,* or *video jockey.* With a lot of brio, Patty introduces Latino and *salsa* videos and answers e-mails from fans. The language she uses is *Spanglish,* half English, half Spanish, breaking from one to the other in the course of a sentence.

Here's how her show kicked off on the day we visited the studios of LATV.

PATTY LOPEZ: *Qué hora es? Es la hora de la buena música aquí en* Mex 2 the Max. That's right, baby. I hope you guys are sittin' down, because we have an hour—a fun-filled hour for you guys. *Tenemos a la scena de* La Chica Sexy *con los Chicanos de Tijuana de esta noche.*

[What's the time? It's time for good music here on *Mex 2 the Max*. That's right, baby. I hope you guys are sittin' down, because we have an hour—a fun-filled hour for you guys. We have the video of *The Sexy Chick* along with the Tijuana Boys for tonight.]

In one of the regular features of *Mex 2 the Max* Patty Lopez reads out e-mails from fans and viewers who want to request a special song. This one came from someone called Angel:

ANGEL'S E-MAIL: *Estaba cambiando los canales, y miré su programa y se me hizo muy interesante.* I would like to ask you to play "El Gavilán" *se llama* Ricardo Cerda. Thanks and good luck. Love ya always, Angel.
[While channel surfing, I saw your program and found it very interesting. I would like to ask you to play "The Sparrow," sung by Ricardo Cerda. Thanks and good luck. Love ya always, Angel.]

Patty says a lot of Latin people come to the States—"I mean we are everywhere!"—who might not feel comfortable speaking English, and "we are putting it out there for them." She says, "I think it's going to be mandatory for people to have to learn Spanish, because it's going to be the second language of the States." Her father is seventy-two and doesn't speak English, "because you know that you can get by not speaking it here."

We left Patty plugging *La Chica Sexy*, the mildest of erotic videos, in which buffoonish men leered at a woman prancing about in a bikini and got bopped by their wives.

Spanglish is not the only Spanish-English hybrid. Linguist Carmen Fought has been studying Chicano, one of the street talks in Latino Los Angeles. She says, "Chicano English is a dialect of English that grew out of the historical contact between English and Spanish in the Southwest. You get articles written that say that Chicano English is just a step on the way to mastery of English. And that's not true at all. Chicano English is now its own vibrant, thriving dialect. It's not going anywhere."

There is also a Chicano Spanish, Spanish with heavy and literal borrowings from English. *Te llamar para trás* is a literal translation of the English phrase *I'll call you back,* which Carmen described as very awkward Spanish that would not be used by Spanish speakers elsewhere. Her research has concentrated on Chicano English, much of it among high-school students who had Spanish-speaking parents.

Carmen says that the way Chicano English developed tells us something about language, cognition, and the human brain. Mexican immigrants learned English as a second language, an accented variety that included sounds and other patterns from their first language, Spanish. Their children, however, grew up speaking both languages. They used the "learner English" of their parents as a basis for developing a new, native dialect of English. Carmen Fought believes that the emergence of Chicano is similar in some ways to the development of pidgins and creoles.

She took us to a nearby park, to watch some kids playing touch football in the sunshine of a late afternoon and to listen to the conversation of two boys who were watching from a park bench. At first they were impossible to understand, their voices rising and falling in a way that was unmistakably Hispanic. The word *fool* sounded like *fooh,* and the word *hotness* was pronounced like *highness.* But after a while our ears grew more attuned to Michael (interestingly, not José) and Jesse. Here is a sample:

MICHAEL: So wassup, dawg? What's cracking, dawg? What's crackin' tomorrow?

JESSE: Barbecue.

MICHAEL:	Yeah. Wassup, man? We gonna throw a party? Wassup?
JESSE:	What girls you gonna have over there?
MICHAEL:	Man, all I'm saying, all I know is that there's gonna be a bunch of primas there.
JESSE:	What about the, what about the party you took Mark to? Mark Ramirez.
MICHAEL:	Southgate?
JESSE:	Yeah, Southgate.
MICHAEL:	That's his family, fool.
JESSE:	Nah, you serious?
MICHAEL:	There's a bunch of hotness over there.
JESSE:	Nah.

Carmen said words like *wassup* and some other features are shared by Chicano and African American English. The Chicano term *hotness* means *good-looking girls*.

JESSE:	What about these fools? Think they're gonna grow up to be some real football or what?
MICHAEL:	Man, that little short fool with cutoff sleeves, he's my cousin, dawg. He might probably be something.

Carmen said the use of *fool* is very common, and occasionally when she was doing fieldwork "they would actually call me *fool*. You know, just kind of slipping it in there the same way we might use *man* or *guy*." Many people believe that Chicano is spoken by people whose first language is Spanish and who don't speak English. But Jesse doesn't in fact speak Spanish. "Only enough to throw in a few words, and those words actually tend to be taboo or swear words usually, when kids just know a few Spanish words."

This is the classic pattern, that the first generation born in the United States will often retain the home language, but by the second generation born here the home language is very often lost.

Carmen vigorously refutes the claim by Vicente Fox and Carlos Fuentes that Latinos are achieving a linguistic reconquest of America. Fuentes may be a great writer, she says, but neither he nor Vicente Fox has done research on language spread and change. They are not experts on the subject. She says that all of the linguists who have studied the subject, without exception, say that by the second generation born here of Mexican-born ancestors, Spanish is 50 percent gone. By the third generation, Spanish is 100 percent gone. People are misled into thinking that Spanish is becoming dominant because, unlike immigration by other groups, which came in waves that began and ended, the Hispanic migration is a continuous flow. So there are always newly arrived Spanish speakers who give the impression of dominating a region or part of a city. In fact, they are assimilating at the same generational rate as other language groups.

She said it was fascinating to see a young man who looks Mexican, looks very much like someone who people will think speaks Spanish, and who speaks in a rhythm that sounds as though he speaks Spanish, but who, when you ask, will say he knows no Spanish—not even enough to order a *burrito* in a takeout-food place.

In her research, Carmen found that speakers in the Mexican American community were losing Spanish very rapidly. Some of them were disappointed about that, but many had come into school when they were five or six years old, speaking Spanish only; by high school, when they were seventeen or eighteen, they had lost it completely. English was completely dominant.

"So," Carmen concluded, "I don't think that Spanish is a threat to English in any way. I think, if anything, it's Spanish that is in danger and that we might want to look out for."

Although other factors may be involved, the census data from 1990 and 2000 appear to document what she observes. Take three cities with large Hispanic populations in Texas:

In San Antonio, in 1990, among children five to seventeen years old, 108,885 said they "speak only English." By 2000, that group had grown by 36 percent, to 148,596. Of Spanish speakers of the same ages, in 1990, 48,188 said they "speak English very well." By 2000, the figure was 54,230, an increase of 12 percent.

For people in San Antonio aged eighteen to sixty-four, there was similar growth in English speaking over the decade. Thus, across a large range of ages, the number of people who spoke only English increased in a decade, as did the numbers of Spanish speakers who spoke English very well.

Dallas and Houston receive more fresh Mexican immigrants than San Antonio, but the census data from those cities do not show dramatic gains for Spanish. In Dallas the number of people under seventeen who spoke only English fell by 2 percent from 1990 to 2000, but in Houston that number rose by 6 percent. Spanish speakers who spoke English "very well" increased in Dallas by 79 percent, in Houston by 58 percent. Among people aged eighteen to sixty-four, the number of those who spoke only English fell by 6 percent in Dallas over the decade, in Houston by 2 percent. But among older people who spoke Spanish at home but spoke English "very well," the figures favored English, increasing in Dallas by 58 percent and in Houston by 51 percent. So the census data do not provide evidence of a massive shift away from English acquisition, the first step in becoming assimilated.

* * *

Let us return to *La Cucaracha*, the nationally syndicated comic strip created by Lalo Alcaraz, a thirty-eight-year-old resident of Los Angeles, who says he carries a "huge chip on his shoulder" from his *pocho* upbringing. *Pocho* means a Mexican born in the United States and considered by real Mexicans to be so assimilated that they call him "American." Alcaraz says he's not Mexican enough for his relatives in Mexico, and not American enough for some in the United States. But there is a certain symbolism in the fact that he writes the sharp dialogue for his young Latino cartoon characters not in Spanish, or Spanglish, or Chicano, but mostly standard American English, and that to access past news stories about the cartoon on the Internet you are instructed to "Click aki."

* * *

Whatever the disagreements between the political scientists and the linguists, one statistic is indisputable. In 2003, Hispanics passed African Americans as the largest minority in the country. Given rates of immigration and natural increase, that disparity is likely to grow. As Hispanics become more influential culturally, economically, and politically, what will the consequences be for America's blacks, who still face their own challenges and discrimination over language?

six

Bad-mouthing Black English

The inner cities of America—the term is often a euphemism for black ghettos—can look very different from one another. Harlem, with its stock of once-grand New York brownstones, has a different appearance from Watts in Los Angeles, with its small, one-story houses surrounded by chain-link fences. But these communities with heavy concentrations of African Americans often have many features in common: poor-quality housing, private or public; high rates of unemployment, school truancy, and dropouts, of drug dealing and abuse, of illegitimate births, of violent crime; and an absence of adult males, because such disproportionate numbers of them, relative to white communities, are in jail. The black communities share similar rates of poverty. In 2002, one in four African American households lived below the federal poverty level. In New York County, where Harlem is located, it was one in three; in Los Angeles County, one black household in five.

These communities also have in common a vibrant culture and language, Black English, which lies at the vital center of that culture. But language may also be a factor in perpetuating the social morbidity—for instance, why 27 percent of blacks fail to graduate from high school, compared with 16 percent of whites; and why only 14 percent of blacks get a college degree, compared with 26 percent of whites.

It is one of the paradoxes of American life that white America both is fascinated by black culture and disapproves of it, embracing it and *bad-mouthing* it simultaneously. The very word *bad-mouth* carries in itself a miniature history of Black English. According to linguist Geneva Smitherman of Michigan State University, *bad-mouthing* came from the West African language Mandingo: *da jugu* meant "slander, abuse," literally "bad mouth." Now it is one of many words white America has borrowed from Black English. Professor Smitherman's book *Black Talk* gives seventeen hundred "words and phrases from the Hood to the Amen Corner" (the neighborhood to the corner of a church where older women frequently say "amen"), and almost one in ten has "crossed over" into general American usage.

Even as it borrows, however, white America continues to *bad-mouth* the source, the dialect that linguists call African American Vernacular English. It has been called "this appalling English dialect . . . gutter slang . . . the dialect of the pimp, the idiom of the gang-banger and the street thug." Not only white commentators but middle-class African Americans have often been as negative. Yet this is the speech of millions of Americans in inner cities all over the United States, a speech that is remarkably consistent from place to place, more consistent than the speech of white Americans from city to city. An African American in Detroit will sound much more like his *soul brothers* in Philadelphia and Los Angeles than will the white inhabitants of the same cities. Black English has become a national form of speech. Its common features—such as *he start* for *he starts; we going* instead of *we are going;* and *we be going* for a habitual action—can be heard everywhere. Those features, and many subtler ones, are the speech of the urban ghettos. They are also increasingly often being appropriated by some Hispanic and Asian Americans, and by middle-class white youths finding a covert prestige or generational protest in imitating black speech.

So little attention had been paid to the language of America's black population that in the 1920s H. L. Mencken could seriously claim,

"The Negro dialect, as we know it today, seems to have been formulated by the song writers for minstrel shows." Mencken meant the attempts to render black speech in writing, calling it "a vague and artificial lingo which had little relation to the actual speech of the Southern blacks."

A great deal of attention has subsequently been paid by linguists, especially after World War II, but the origins of black speech have only been partially uncovered.

The first generation of research surmised that blacks' speech derived from pieces of dialects brought by their slave owners from different parts of England. One example would be the use of *axe* instead of *ask*. Frederic G. Cassidy, editor of the *Dictionary of American Regional English*, notes that in Old English the word was *acsian* but over time the "ks" sound was reversed. The old verb *axe* appears fully conjugated in Chaucer's *Troilus and Criseyde—axe, axen, axed*. More than four centuries later, in the novels of Anthony Trollope, *axe* appears in the mouths of country squires speaking their local Barchester dialect. In fact, *axe* was used by Southern white speakers until recent years, when it fell out of favor because it had become such a marker for black speech.

When linguists tried systematically to match English dialect forms with patterns of colonial migration and slaveholding, the *Anglicist theory* fell apart. It was supplanted by the *creole theory*, that African American English is a descendant of English pidgins developed during the slave trade. Pidgins passed on to another generation to become creoles.

In *The Story of English*, we followed this theory back to its origins in West Africa, to Mambolo, a trading post up the Great Scearcies River in Sierra Leone. British and American slavers working up rivers like this introduced the English language to the African middlemen from whom they bought the slaves. Three hundred years ago, blacks and whites communicated in a simplified English known as *pidgin*. This Anglo-African mixture is still the lingua franca on the river, as we heard from the boatmen on the dock touting for passengers to Freetown, shouting,

"Freetown-Freetown-Freetown, now-now-now-now," and, "Verygood-verygood-verygood." Navigating through the sandbanks, the captain told the helmsman, "Go small-small," for "very slow."

Near the coast, on Bunce Island, are the ruins of an old fort where newly captured slaves were penned up. To prevent revolts, traders mixed slaves who spoke different African languages. The traders spoke to them in pidgin English, and the slaves used and elaborated it to speak among themselves. So, even before they left Africa in the infamous slave ships, they were speaking a version of English that was all their own.

John Baugh, a Stanford University linguist, himself African American, said that these "are the very origins of contemporary African American English."

We also filmed on the Sea Islands off South Carolina—Kiawah, Edisto, Daufuskie, and Wadmalaw—low-lying barrier islands, sandy on the seaward side, wooded and marshy toward the mainland. Once, rice and cotton were grown on plantations here. An infestation of the boll weevil killed the cotton in the 1920s, and the islanders now survive on general farming, fishing, and a lot of vacationing mainlanders. The novelist Pat Conroy taught school for a year on Daufuskie and described its fictional representation, Yamacraw, like this:

> The island is fringed with the green, undulating marshes of the southern coast; shrimp boats ply the waters around her and fishermen cast their lines along her bountiful shores. Deer cut through her forests in small, silent herds. The great southern oaks stand broodingly on her banks. The island and the waters around her teem with life. There is something eternal and indestructible about the tide-eroded shores and the dark threatening silences of the swamps in the heart of the island.

This was where people spoke Gullah, one of the early precursors of today's African American Vernacular, and twenty years ago you could still hear faint whispers of that original slave English. Older people, such as Benjamin Bligen and his sister Janie Hunter, were among the last natural Gullah speakers. Benjamin, who was mending his seine net before going fishing for *ashtas* (oysters) and *rustys* (crabs), sat with Janie in the shade of those old trees as we listened to their conversation:

JANIE:	All these trees here are medicine.
BENJAMIN:	Yeah, yeah.
JANIE:	We're sat down 'neath medicine right now.
BENJAMIN:	Yeah, yeah.
JANIE:	All them was medicine. I'm looking at medicine ever' day.
BENJAMIN:	Yeah. Like molasses.
JANIE:	White root.
BENJAMIN:	All them things.
JANIE:	Big girl. Red oak fire.
BENJAMIN:	Yeah, yeah.
JANIE:	All those was medicine.
BENJAMIN:	Oh yeah.
JANIE:	Papa had a whole bag full. He'd say, "Go in the loft, get a piece of bark, and give it to drink."
BENJAMIN:	Go to bed with fever, wake up in the mornin', fever gone.
JANIE:	Fever gone, boy. Done sweat that fever out.
BENJAMIN:	Oh yeah.
JANIE:	Oh, they was good time.
BENJAMIN:	Good times, good times.
JANIE:	Good times. They time is still here right now. But they, they just don't want to own it.
BENJAMIN:	Oh yeah.
JANIE:	But I still old-time and I'll keep my old time here.

BENJAMIN: Oh yeah.

JANIE: Nothing like it.

BENJAMIN: Give me that old-time religion.

We left them singing "Give Me That Old Time Religion"—voices from the past, because today both brother and sister have passed on, and Gullah is kept alive only as a cultural artifact and tourist attraction, no longer a living language.

How the original slave speech or plantation creole developed depended on the period, location, and circumstances of slave management. Linguists Guy Bailey and Patricia Cukor-Avila write that in the colonial period black slaves and white indentured servants often worked together, and relationships between the races were more fluid than later. There were differences in the Upper and Lower South, slaves who were nearer the coast in the Lower South, the location of the largest plantations, often having minimal contact with whites. After the Revolution, more than 10 percent of the slaves in the Upper South were freed, and for the rest restrictions were relaxed, so there was more racial contact. Then, in 1793, the cotton gin was invented, and that led to a huge growth in cotton production. Cultivation spread west into Mississippi and Texas and led to a dramatic increase in the importation of slaves. This "cotton kingdom" was characterized by very large plantations with big slave populations working the fields. When slavery ended, this society was the source of many of the most important products of African American Vernacular culture—for instance, blues, jazz, and rock-and-roll music.

After the Civil War, the plantation system was replaced by share-cropping and tenant farming, for blacks and whites, and the emergence of general stores as the anchor of the Southern economy. In these stores, both races mingled to buy tools and provisions, and to secure credit against their future crops. Then industrialization began, the Jim

Crow laws were passed, and the races were again segregated. By the early twentieth century, frustrated blacks began migrating north to what they called "the Promised Land."

One community in East Central Texas has changed little since the days of tenant farming and has been the focus of intensive research by Bailey and Cukor-Avila for clues to the evolution of modern Black English. We reached what they called "Springville" after driving across miles of flatland, past the mesmerizing blur of furrows recently plowed in soil enriched by periodic flooding of the Brazos River. In winter it is cold; in summer, stiflingly hot. Because there are few trees and no hills, you can see for miles, as you can hear the whistles of the endless trains carrying freight for the Southern Pacific and Union Pacific Railroads. Springville is a tiny community now, sandwiched between two lines, trembling every few minutes as the trains rumble through.

The same family has owned the redbrick general store for more than a century, and it appears hardly to have changed. A cast-iron stove sits in the middle, for fires on freezing winter days, when customers, black and white, would linger for the warmth. On a slight elevated platform are a nineteenth-century desk and an ancient contraption that holds the accounts of customers. Dusty showcases display a modest selection of groceries, notions, and dry goods. At the back is the small post office. The store appears caught in a time warp.

It was here that Patricia Cukor-Avila, of the University of North Texas, conducted her early research nearly two decades ago. Rarely does linguistic research in any one community extend over such a long period of time, and to achieve this, she said, it was necessary to win the trust of the locals: "When I first started out with this project, I would basically hang out there most of the day and interact with people who came in and talk with them, not necessarily record right at first, until I got to know people. The mail is still delivered at the store—there is no mail delivery. So that always ensured a nice crowd of people coming in about the time that the mail would be brought to the store and then put up into the various postal boxes. People oftentimes don't just come to get their mail and leave. They come, get their mail, sit down, open it, sit around, and talk."

By concentrating in this way, she and Bailey have been able to look at how speech changes over time in a single community. Over time in the case of Springville meant an extraordinary chance to hear voices that literally go back to the days of slavery, and the changes since. In the 1930s and early 1940s, workers from the Works Progress Administration made a series of recordings and photographs in this part of Texas. Among their subjects were elderly black people who were born into slavery in the United States, the children or grandchildren of slaves brought directly from Africa. Although the legal slave trade ended in 1808, Bailey says that didn't end the illegal importation of slaves. In *The Emergence of Black English*, editors Bailey, Cukor-Avila, and Natalie Maynor argue that illegal importation was heaviest in the cotton lands from the Mississippi Delta to Texas. One of the former slaves interviewed by the WPA was born in Liberia, captured there in the 1850s, and brought to Texas as a child.

It is haunting to look at the photos of these black people, their work-worn bodies in shabby clothing, yet their faces to us expressing a dignity that seems to be absent from the faces of some of the gaunt, half-starved white migrants in the famous photographs of the dust-bowl victims of the same Depression years. Suddenly slavery advances out of the "long ago" to within living memory, an impression reinforced by listening to people's voices.

One WPA interviewee was Laura Smalley of Hempstead, Texas, south of Springville, in the same river country, known as Brazos Bottom. Laura was born to a slave mother imported from Mississippi; she said she was nine when "freedom broke," her term for the Emancipation Proclamation of 1863. Lincoln's proclamation freeing slaves in the

Confederate states, in the middle of the Civil War, was issued on January 1; the slaves in Texas were not told of it until June. She said, "All of them went to the house to see old master. An' I thought old master was dead, but he wasn'. . . . He had been off to the war, an' come back. All the niggers gathered aroun' to see ol' master again. You know, an' ol' master didn' tell, you know, they was free. . . . They worked there, I think now they say they worked them six months after that, six months. And turn them loose on the nineteen of June. That's why, you know, they celebrate that day. Colored folks celebrates that day."

It is true that in Texas June 19—or Juneteenth, as they call it—was a bigger holiday for blacks than the Fourth of July and is still widely celebrated.

Laura's descriptions of slave life were graphic, like this scene when a house slave known as Aunt M was accused by her mistress of hurting her when she took her by the wrists and made her sit in a rocking chair. Laura recounted what happened when the master came home and his wife complained the slave had hurt her.

An' he ask her then, says, "What you doing in this house here, hurting her ol' mistress?" Say, "She wasn't hurting no ol' mistress, she was jus', when mistress started whoop her, she sat her down." But they taken that ol' woman, poor ol' woman, carried her in the peach orchard an' whipped her. An' you know, jus' tied her han' this-a-way, you know, 'roun' the peach orchard tree, I can remember that jus' as well, look like to me I can, and 'roun' the tree an' whipped her. You know, she couldn' do nothing but jus' kick her feet, you know, jus' kick her feet. But they jus' had her clothes off down to her wais', you know. They didn' have her plum[b] naked, but they had her clothes down to her waist. An' every now and then they'd whip her, you know, an' then snuff the pipe out on her, you know, jus' snuff pipe out on her. You know, the embers in the pipe. . . . Man, he sure did whip her. Well, he whipped her so that at night they had to grease her back, grease her back. . . . Later that evening they give her her dinner. Lay there and watch, she was whipped so bad, you know, she din' want to eat, you know. If they whip you half a day, you ain't want to eat. Not at all. No.

In transcribing the accounts of such barbarity, the researchers were intrigued to notice how different this speech was from current African American Vernacular English. Bailey said, "In some respects the syntax and grammar were more similar to white speech of the time." Many of the features common to contemporary Black English are absent from the "slave" tapes, for instance, what linguists call "the invariant *be*," as in *they be working,* and the "deleted copula," leaving out the auxiliary verb in *they working.*

Bailey and Cukor-Avila interviewed people of several generations living in Springville in the 1980s and 1990s, using pseudonyms, as they did with "Willy," who grew up on a farm close to the store and worked in agriculture all his life. Patricia said he was "a very good example of what we would call older African American speech patterns." We recorded a conversation between Willy and Guy Bailey.

GUY: You told me that when you were a little boy you did a lot of hunting and stuff.

WILLY: Yuh, I hunted a little bit, yuh.

GUY: What all'dya hunt?

WILLY: Armadillo, rabbit, and anything I could catch!

GUY: Is that right? Is the armadillo pretty good to eat?

WILLY: Yessir, he good, sir.

GUY: I've never had armadillo. What's it taste like?

WILLY: Taste good. Like chicken.

GUY:	Is that right?
WILLY:	Yessir. You cook it right, sir.
GUY:	Is that right? How d'you cook it?
WILLY:	Well, sir, my momma she boil him. Boil him. In a pot, you know.
GUY:	Uh huh.
WILLY:	Put some onion rind in, make gravy, fry him.

And Willy concluded, "Hard times in my day. Yessir. We work hard, sir." The researchers found that the speech of older black people like Willy also lacked the features of modern city Black English and more resembled the Southern white speech of their time. Here is an example of some dialogue recorded by Cukor-Avila in the general store between Rupert, born in 1916, and Slim, born in 1932, both African Americans. Rupert was well known locally for stories about his encounters with a ghost, the "Little Man."

SLIM:	It's a little man that follows him aroun'. A little short man. He ask him for cigarettes an' things.
RUPERT:	Oh jus' about that tall. He followed me one night. Right over there. Clean to the house . . . An' uh, I didn't see anythin'. I started turnin' in the yar'. Here comes somethin' followin' behin' me. I turned aroun' an' there he standin' right in the middle of the yar'. "What's your name? You'd better tell me your name." I said, "Come up on me I'm gonna cut ya!" . . . Me an' uh, me an' ol' Moses was sittin' over there. Moses went back to the highway. I said, "Who is that?" Moses said, "Oh that's a dog." No that wasn' no dog. I

said, "That was human being!" Moses said, "Oh yes! Most those devils are human!"

But the younger the Springville African Americans they studied, the more the speech began to resemble urban black speech of today. Patricia Cukor-Avila compared thirty-two grammatical features in the speech patterns of whites and blacks in the periods 1920–40, 1940–60, and after 1960. One notable feature that is easy for nonlinguists to grasp is the use of "s" on the third person singular of verbs. Among black speakers of the earlier periods, like Rupert and Slim above, the use of the "s" (as in *he goes to work*) is typical; it starts to shift in the next generation, and is gone in the speech of Springville residents born after 1960. The youngest were saying things like, *His sister go where she need to go.* Cukor-Avila describes this as a "new development" within the African American Vernacular English grammatical system. Besides the loss of the "s," other innovations are the use of *be* plus a verb in the present participle—for example, *he be working*—and the use of *had* plus a past-tense verb, as in *Yesterday I had went,* or *Yesterday I had saw him;* these features were not found in black speech before World War II.

These insights led Bailey and Cukor-Avila to conclude that urban black speech appeared to be diverging from rather than converging with white speech, as a result of the great black migration to the North. Starting during World War I, which created a Northern demand for black labor, and lasting until the 1970s, some six million blacks left the rural South for the major cities of the North. There whites and blacks did not mix. In fact, the movement of Southern blacks into city centers often started "white flight" to the suburbs, creating black ghettos. Bailey said, "In the large cities you had spatial segregation but you also had the formation of separate communities often with a kind of oppositional culture to the rest of the U.S. This created an ideal context for African American Vernacular English to develop along a sort of separate track."

Here are some examples of the product of that separate development. They were collected by John Baugh in his fieldwork. This is a black man of sixty-two:

> Inside of you, you gotta mind. There's a mind that be workin' that's constant, that never sleep . . . it's yo subconscious mind, which never go to sleep on you. Because . . . I think when it's gone, you done lef' the world anyway. But your subconscious mind is steady workin'. This is why men don' live as long as womens because there is so much that's pressin' on you. And this is why that black people is hypertension; more of us die from high blood pressure because of that strain. We live under that shit constant. . . . It's no black person livin' free in the United States; I don' care how rich he is.

Some other examples were collected by John Baugh in Philadelphia and Los Angeles.

> When the baby be sleep, and the othe' kids be at school, and my husband be at work, then . . . I might can finally sit down.

> She told David they Mama had went to Chicago to see her sister and her sister's new baby.

> If he lay a hand on my kid again, I'll be done killed that motherfucker.

Bailey believes that white and black grammars "are very different today, probably more different than they've ever been. And their phonologies [sound systems] aren't very similar either; it's a kind of independent development." William Labov of Philadelphia says that today "the African American community are carried even further away on a separate current of grammatical change . . . as a consequence of the large and increasing residential segregation of African Americans in Northern cities."

To speak of black "grammar" will disconcert many Americans, white or black, who think that Black English is merely a lazy or broken English. *Washington Post* columnist William Raspberry once called it "a language that has no right or wrong expressions, no consistent spellings or pronunciations, and no discernible rules." That is a common assumption, except among linguists. In 1969, William Labov analyzed the speech of blacks in Philadelphia and in Harlem and concluded that Black English had a consistent internal structure, grammar, and syntax. Linguist John Baugh wrote that Labov's research, "The Logic of Nonstandard English," "was the single most important article ever written that debunked the pervasive linguistic fallacies associated with cognitive-deficit hypotheses"—that is, the fallacy that speakers of Black English were somehow mentally backward. In 1997, Labov told a Senate hearing: "This African American Vernacular English is a dialect of English, which shares most of the grammar and vocabulary with other dialects of English. But it is distinctively different in many ways, and more different from standard English than any other dialect spoken in Continental North America. It is not a set of slang words, or a random set of grammatical mistakes, but a well formed set of rules of grammar and pronunciation that is capable of conveying complex logic and reasoning."

There is still a dispute, too specialized for nonlinguists like us, over whether the *creole theory* of black linguistic development means there is a deeply embedded structure in black language or whether, in Cukor-Avila's words, "factors such as education, age, and social class were also significant in determining linguistic choices."

*   *   *

We left Springville with the sobering realization that a hundred, even fifty years ago, rural blacks and whites sounded more alike than we might have thought. Today, whites and inner-city blacks sound more different than we might have hoped. After decades of genuine civil-rights advances, and significant achievements by the growing black middle class, the majority of African Americans and white society are growing further apart, because more separate languages mean more separate peoples.

That is where we come back to the fascinating paradox. Whatever its evolution, urban black culture has from its earliest days had a profound influence on the popular culture of white America. Over a century of musical innovation—with ragtime, jazz, the blues, boogie-woogie, doo-wop, soul, rock and roll, and today hip-hop—generations of white Americans have embraced the black imagination, millions as avid consumers, some as crossover artists like Elvis Presley or the contemporary Eminem. John McWhorter, another Stanford University linguist, who is also African American, calls black sound, especially after the 1960s, "the cross-racial bedrock of the American musical sensibility."

In the process of borrowing this sensibility, white America has also appropriated a lot of Black English Vernacular, whether slang or the code-speak that was part of Black English development from slavery days to keep whites, so to speak, in the dark. As the writer James Baldwin noted: "There was a moment in time and in this place when my brother, or my mother, or my father, or my sister had to convey to me, for example, the danger in which I was standing from the white man standing just behind me, and to convey this with speed and in a language the white man could not possibly understand, and that, indeed, he cannot understand today." Baldwin had some ironic observations on how white Americans considered it *hip* or *hep* to pick up black expressions:

> Now, I do not know what white Americans would sound like if there had never been any black people in the United States, but they would not sound the way they sound. Jazz, for example, is

a very specific sexual term, as in *jazz me, baby*, but white people purified it into the Jazz Age. *Sock it to me, baby*, which means, roughly, the same thing, has been adopted by Nathaniel Hawthorne's descendants with no qualms or hesitations at all, along with *let it all hang out* and *right on! Beat to his socks*, which was once the black's most total and despairing image of poverty, was transformed into a thing called the Beat Generation, which phenomenon was, largely, composed of "upright" middle class white people, imitating poverty, trying to *get down*, to *get with it*, doing their despairing best to be *funky*, which we the blacks never dreamed of doing—we *were funky*, baby, like *funk* was going out of style.

Many other borrowings from blacks have enriched American English—dance names such as *cakewalk* (the 2003 invasion of Iraq would be a *cakewalk*, according to some in the Bush administration), *jitterbug, break dancing*. To be *cool*, or *heavy*, became universally American. One wave of popularity for black idiom among whites came in the 1920s and 1930s, when it was *cool* for New Yorkers to go to Harlem to hear jazz greats like Duke Ellington and Louis Armstrong but also the *hepcat* Cab Calloway, who created a "Jive Talk Dictionary" in song, popularizing expressions such as *hip* (wise, sophisticated), *in the groove* (perfect), *square* (unhip), and *chick* (girl), or *a hip chick* (a beautiful girl). But the white *hepcats* drifted away, and Harlem became slum territory for decades after World War II, only beginning to enjoy a renaissance in the 1990s, when soaring Manhattan real-estate values made it desirable. That trend was symbolized when Bill Clinton chose to locate his post-presidential office in Harlem.

But there is the other side to the black-white language paradox. Despite its enormous influence in popular culture, what is clear to black Americans and to any sensitive whites is that inner-city Black English, whatever its evolution, is a huge barrier to advancement in American society, limiting prospects in education, employment, and housing. For years Stanford University linguist John Baugh has been studying what he calls "linguistic profiling," as real in black lives as the "racial profiling" whereby skin color alone makes police suspect criminality.

We joined Baugh in Detroit, home of Motown in the 1960s, today boasting a thriving hip-hop scene. The white rapper Eminem comes from the Detroit area called 8-Mile, the title of his signature movie. Inner-city Detroit is 82 percent African American, but language can define you as well as the color of your skin.

At the Greyhound bus station, John Baugh demonstrated the technique he's used for years to reveal how Americans react to different ethnic accents. He checks the rental-housing section in the local paper, and then calls to inquire about places advertised. He calls first using an African American accent, then again using a Latino speech pattern, and a third time in a neutral American accent, which is in fact how he really talks. In general, results from this effort in many cities show that those with minority dialects do not fare so well, particularly in affluent communities. The outcome reflects white perceptions of both race and economic class, but also prejudice based on how people speak.

Baugh sees both sides of this, having felt the pull both ways: "At a young age, then, I received mixed messages about language; some were overt, advocating that I 'speak properly' and avoid 'bad language,' whereas others were more subtle, reflected by the hippest Sisters and Brothers who emphatically rejected 'white speech.' . . . I didn't want to sound 'lame' and, as I had observed 'on the corner,' most of the 'cool brothers' could 'talk the talk'—and those who exhibited urban eloquence *never* did so in standard English."

The two dialects clash particularly in America's schools. Ann Arbor, an hour from Detroit, was the scene of what became a landmark court case about prejudice against Black English. In 1979, the mothers of a handful of black kids at the largely white school claimed they were not being educated because of their language. When they spoke as they did at home, their teachers assumed they couldn't do schoolwork. Ironically, the school was named after Martin Luther King, Jr. Annie Blair, one of the mothers, had moved north from Tennessee. She told us, "When my kids was tested and was put into special-ed classes and I felt like that they were not getting educated and was not treated equally. And I felt like that shouldn't be a barrier because of the language to stop them from being educated." One of her sons, Asheen, now a man in his thirties, said, "They sort of felt like we were unteachable, in a sense. So it kind of made them go towards other students more and gave them a little bit more help than they would give us. Actually, to be honest, the teachers really didn't communicate with us too much. It was just sort of like, in a sense, that we were on our own."

A social worker, Ruth Zweifler, familiar with the housing project the boys came from, became convinced that they were being discriminated against because of their African American English: "There were maybe twenty-four poor black children in a sea of affluent white families and they really were having a very hard time. Language is the marker for assumed attitudes—coming with an implied criticism, which is what I think a black child carries with him. We as adults, as mainstream society, as Americans, have really done bad by these little kids."

Unable to make any headway with the school board, Ruth contacted lawyers in Detroit, and together they thrashed out a legal strategy that led to a landmark court decision on Black English. One of the lawyers, Ken Lewis, said they tried at first to focus on the children's poverty, but "there is really no constitutional right not to be poor in this country." Eventually they were able to tie language to race as a barrier to education. And they were victorious. John Baugh said the most significant thing raised during the trial "was that you had a federal judge acknowledge formally that African American Vernacular English represented a significant barrier to academic achievement and success. He confirmed that the school district was really insensitive to the linguistic background of the vast majority of African American students within the school district."

The judge ordered the district to make a plan to teach black students, and the school district announced that teachers at the Martin Luther King School would have to take sensitivity courses.

Ken Lewis said, "One of the things I remember Judge Joyner indicating in his opinion was the need to help youngsters appreciate the difference between the language of the majority, how it would impact upon your being perceived by others."

The judgment brought mixed reactions even from blacks. William Raspberry of the *Washington Post* approvingly quoted one of the plaintiff lawyers: "When a 5-year-old has his language system treated as inferior from his first day of school, the resulting psychological damage is inevitable. Once this barrier is raised by school officials, the child begins to withdraw and his learning performance suffers." But the case got no sympathy from an equally influential black columnist, Carl T. Rowan, who said he found the ruling "far fetched." Rowan wrote that he would remain skeptical "until we make more black parents understand the value of reading in the home, until more teachers force ghetto students to read newspapers and magazines, and at least try to resist peer-group pressures to downgrade standard English. 'My teacher was insensitive to my black English' is an alibi that black youngsters can use forever to 'explain' why they did not aspire to excellence, and thus never learned to read—or to prepare for a decent life."

From Paris, where he had long exiled himself to escape racial friction, James Baldwin wrote to the *New York Times:* "A child cannot be taught by anyone who despises him, and a child cannot afford to be fooled. A child cannot be taught by anyone whose demeanor, essentially, is that the child repudiate his experience and all that gives him sustenance and enter a limbo in which he will no longer be black, and in which he knows that he can never become white. Black people have lost too many children that way."

And Baldwin added: "The argument has nothing to do with language itself but with the role of language. Language, incontestably, reveals the speaker. . . . It goes without saying, then, that language is also a political instrument, means, and proof of power. It is the most vivid and crucial key to identity. It reveals the private identity, and connects one with, or divorces one from, the larger public, or communal identity."

Years later, in 1997, the argument Ken Lewis had used successfully in court was raised by educators in Oakland, California. They claimed, however, that Black English, for which they resurrected the old term *Ebonics,* was not a dialect of English but a separate language. That caused a national storm. Critics felt, in the words of John Baugh, that the Oakland School Board "was trying to abscond with the limited bilingual education funding available for students for whom English is not native." Baugh said that if Education Secretary Riley had not squashed that separate-language notion instantly, "countless school districts from across the country would have quickly lined up at the federal Title VII trough."

But the storm had another side. Well-educated blacks joined whites in believing that the Oakland authorities wanted to *teach* Black English, and the commentators unleashed a stream of hostility. Liberal columnists referred to Black English as "gibberish . . . the patois of America's meanest streets . . . a mutant language." Recalling this in an NPR talk, Geoffrey Nunberg said, "It's hard to read those characterizations without feeling that a current of displacement is at work—at least, it's striking how many of the words that critics apply to the dialect in the press are the same ones that many whites apply in private to the people who speak it."

The Ebonics story consumed laymen and the linguistics community.

Dennis Preston talked about it when we met in Pennsylvania. He said that if national columnists who called Black English "gibberish" had used the same kind of language about the intelligence or physical characteristics of an ethnic group like blacks, they would have lost their jobs. "It's pretty horrifying, when you think of it, that we can still describe people who just go about living their daily lives, speaking a language that they learned in their homes and in their neighborhoods, and have some outsider listen to it and say it's 'gibberish,' when it serves them perfectly well as a vehicle of communication for what they want to do in those environments."

Preston, who has studied many European languages, said that in most European countries kids do not go to school speaking the standard language of that country: "It's not true in Italy. It's not true in northern Switzerland, for example—there's a radically different dialect of German. But when those kids go to school the school system says to them: Now, look, when you travel outside of Switzerland or outside of Sicily or, you know, wherever we are, you're going to need standard Italian or standard German. It's not because—and here's the kicker—it's not because it's any better, and it's not because your dialect is dumb or insufficient for the things you do with friends and family. It's just that this variety is more widespread, there's a bigger literature in it, and it's just going to serve you well to learn it. So, for some odd reason, in Europe they don't attack native dialects, they simply equip people with something else, which they think they should have. You can imagine the psychological repercussions of this. The kids who go to school say, 'Oh yeah, something else we got to learn,' rather than, 'Gee whiz, my brothers, my sisters, my friends, my whole family, my aunts, uncles use sloppy speech,' which is in fact what we do to kids in the American educational system."

Oakland schools have put the Ebonics fiasco behind them as the city tries to rebuild itself culturally and physically from the disastrous earthquake of 1989, and tries to cultivate a sense of pride among African

Americans there. Not all young blacks share the civic optimism. We spent an evening with a talented young poet, Chinaka Hodge, who performed at a poetry slam. When she was sixteen, her work made her a member of the Berkeley/Oakland team, winners of the National Teen Poetry Slam in 2000, and later won her a scholarship to New York University. She was a recipient of *Teen People* magazine's What's Next Award, and performed at the awards ceremony at Harlem's Apollo Theater. Her poetry uses an interesting mixture of standard and Black English, which she calls *slang*. She told us, "A good deal of youth in the country speak very standard English and another portion speaks the slang, and I think a lot of us run, you know, right down the middle of that gamut."

One of her poems, "Barely Audible," echoes imagery used by the legendary blues singer Billie Holiday in "Strange Fruit," about black lynchings.

> *This is Darius' world*
> *he moves feebly*
> *decrepit in the candy apple neon glow*
> *of Mohammed's Millenium Market*
> *Darius*
> *clutches brown paper bag*
> *all his dreams, packaged at liquor store*
> *his eyes are red*
> *I tell myself its because he don't sleep at night*
> *he's up counting*
> *he knows how many stars are in the sky*
> *he can hear the ocean lapping at the edge of the world*
> *he can tell you how many times it hits the shore*
> *but folks don't ask him things like that*
> *so he counts dubs, counts 8ths*
> *drinks fifths and forties*

on 18th and Myrtle
Darius
He's dying beneath billboards for DeBeers
Wants to put diamonds in his teeth
He counts rocks
And sniffs sacks of cum
On easy Fridays
Its 3:30
He'll soon be dangling from streetlight like strange fruit
from poplar trees.

Asked about the imagery, Chinaka says, "It's our generation's sadness. There's not as many, you know, lynchings going on as, you know, in Billie Holiday's time, but at the same time there's a lot of death that's going unnoticed and a lot of black folks are dying in Oakland. So, I mean, it's not the same death but its important anyway, it's important, and just as urgent, if not more."

That ability to use the black vernacular creatively while mastering standard English is the grail that schools ideally impart to their students—in effect, to create the kind of bilingualism Dennis Preston talked about in Europe.

In Los Angeles, we visited the city's most listened-to morning drive-time radio host, Steve Harvey, a handsome and confident man, who wears a gray homburg hat tilted back on his head as he sits at a microphone in a studio overlooking the sprawling city, and talks in his own version of Black English. Like Chinaka Hodge, he calls it *slang*. When we asked jokingly, "Do you speak American?" he laughed and said, "I speak good enough American. You know, I think there's variations of speaking American. I don't think there's any one set way, because America's so diverse. You know, man, regardless as to how I talk, you know, I relax and just let it hang out and flow. Suburban America or upward America is not my audience. My audience is mostly grassroots people. And I sound mostly like they uncle, so. See, like I said, I sound mostly like *they* uncle. And I was cool with that. That sound good to me. *Isn't.* You know, *isn't* is not in my vocabulary. The word *isn't* requires my mouth to stretch in a way that it don't stretch—*isn't*—and then I leave it out there too long, you know, I look really stupid. I actually almost black out when I say that." As far as he is concerned, the correct word is *ain't.*

When he thought about it a bit more, Steve Harvey said, "Well, you know, you do have to be bilingual in this country. Which means you can be very, very adept at slang, but you also have to be adept at getting through a job interview."

Los Angeles school authorities know that their minority students will need to be, in effect, bilingual. Since 1991, sixty schools have been using an experimental program called Academic English Mastery. At PS 100, in Watts, we watched a fifth-grade class going through a drill on the differences between what they termed African American English and Mainstream American English. Then they divided into four teams to play a game like Jeopardy! in which they were awarded points for getting the right answers to language questions.

Daniel Russell, a Korean American teacher, put up a test sentence—*My grandpa cook dinner every night*—and asked, "Which feature is not Mainstream American English?"

One of the kids, named Maiso, said, "Third person singular."

THE TEACHER: And, Maiso, how do you code-switch it into Mainstream American English?

MAISO: *My grandpa cooks dinner every night.*

The teacher said that was right and gave that team five hundred points, and a big cheer went up.

The teacher gave another example: *He funny.* A student said, *"He is funny,"* and the teacher said, "Excellent translation."

Another sentence from the teacher: *We don't have nothin' to do.*

A boy: *"We don't have nothinguh to do."* But the teacher said, "Oh, I'm sorry. That is not an accurate translation into Mainstream American English, so you're at minus two hundred," to groans from the team. He rolled the dice again; the team won another chance and got it right: *"We don't have anything to do."* More points and more cheers. These kids were clearly turned on by the game, and most of the questions they got right.

The director of the project, Noma LeMoine, said they ran into some flak from critics, who thought they were *teaching* African American language, teaching Ebonics, which they don't need to do, because the kids already know it. She said, "Our task is to help move them towards mastery of the language at school, in its oral and written form, but to do that in a way where they are not devalued, or where they feel denigrated in any way by virtue of their cultural and linguistic differences."

When we asked why that was better than telling them it's incorrect, she said, "It's important to validate who they are, their culture, their experiences, their language. Because when you begin to devalue youngsters and make them feel that who they are doesn't count, then we've turned them off on education."

We listened a little longer to the students and the teacher, who put up the sentence *Last night we bake cookies* and asked, "Are you ready? Number one, what language is it in?"

STUDENT: AAL.

TEACHER: It is in African American language. Number two, what linguistic feature is in AAL?

STUDENT: Past-tense marker *-ed*.

TEACHER: Past-tense marker *-ed*. That's cool! And how do you code-switch it to Mainstream American English?

STUDENT: *Last night we baked cookies.*

TEACHER: You got five hundred more points. Is it too easy,

or I just taught you well this year? [This was followed by big cheering.]

Students in the program show significant gains in written English,
and those behind the program would like to extend it to more schools
and to more grades. They believe that unless more teachers treat home
language sympathetically they'll condemn more generations to school
failure. Language remains a formidable frontier in the legacy of slavery.

John Baugh says, "For far too long the quest for racial equity has
pushed hot buttons like affirmative action, while ignoring the importance of corresponding linguistic buttons altogether; that cycle must be
broken if race relations in this country are ever to improve."

His fellow linguist Dennis Preston stressed how hard it is for a person to change his dialect. Americans across the social spectrum have a
real distaste for people who fail to pull themselves up by their bootstraps
linguistically, and don't understand that this bootstrapping is not easy.
In fact, Preston believes it is as difficult as learning a foreign language,
a task most Americans shrink from. Preston says, "Even in schools it
seems to me that teachers believe that kids should just pay attention and
not use what they think of as sloppy speech. But sloppy speech of
course is their native language, and so not to do that requires the acquisition of something else."

Two other linguists, Cecilia Cutler and Renée Blake of the Linguistics Department at New York University, studied the attitudes of teachers in six New York high schools. They concluded that over the past
quarter-century teachers have become more positive in their opinions
about the structure of Black English, but that their attitudes depended
heavily on the philosophy of the school, and on how many black students they had. The more black students these teachers had to deal
with, the less they thought Black English had rules, and the more they
thought it was just a lazy form of English.

These teachers may have encountered what the writer Mark Halpern found when teaching at Richard Green High School for Teaching in New York City. He said that many of his black students became furious and shouted, " 'Who are you trying to be?' when another student used standard English in class." Recounting this in the *New York Times,* Felicia R. Lees said that educators once predicted that, as more black people entered the mainstream, the dialect would fade not only among the middle class, as it has done, but also among the poor. Linguists say, however, that the current generation of inner-city youth relies more heavily on black vernacular than ever. "The persistence of the dialect reflects, in part, the growing resistance of some young blacks to assimilate and their efforts to use language as part of a value system that prizes cultural distinction. It also stems from the increasing isolation of black inner-city residents from both whites and middle-class blacks, and stems as well from a deep cynicism about the payoffs of conforming. While the dialect is used as a kind of in-group code among many blacks of all stations, educators are concerned about those young people who never master standard English at all."

Whatever teachers or the general public think, however, no observer of our general culture can ignore the vitality and appeal of black culture and language for white, especially young white, people.

As rock and roll revolutionized the popular-music culture from the mid-1950s, the hip-hop phenomenon has for this generation, not just in music, dance, and language but in its national commercial exploitation in clothing and accessories. Hip-hop had modest beginnings on the streets of New York and Philadelphia in the late 1970s with a combination of break dancing, graffiti art, or "writing" on city walls and trains, and rappers talking, or *MC-ing,* to a beat from records jerked forward and backward by disk jockeys. In 1983, for *The Story of English,* we filmed a street party in Philadelphia featuring an early group, the Scanner Boys, with two MCs, Perrey P, or Voice Master, and Grandmaster Tone, two artists in a black tradition going all the way back to Africa, to the highly admired "man of words." What is interesting two decades later is how many of their words and expressions have since passed into the general language, in common use among white Americans. The Scanner Boys used *check it out* (pay attention to what's going on), *chill out* and *max out* (be cool and relaxed), *fresh* (good), *that's bad* (it's good), *that's good* (it's bad), *funky fresh* (real, real bad), *wassup* (what's going on), and they called a break dancer they were watching *the hip-hop kid*, the first time we'd heard *hip-hop*.

These expressions would sound stale, too used, to young hip-hop performers today. We visited a group called the Athletic Mic League performing at the Blind Pig club in Ann Arbor. Some of the group are college students, and all speak standard American but use street talk among themselves and for their lyrics. In their dressing room, Wesley Taylor said, "Everything follows the streets in America. So that whatever's going on there, it goes from here to here, then eventually mainstream America, which is, you know, white America."

Their talk is filled with fresh meanings for worlds such as *stacked, live, vibing, sick,* and *ill.* Trey Allen said that when he comes down for the performance, "I'm edgy about what I'm about to walk into. I hope the place is *stacked*. I hope that the audience is *live*. I hope when I step out this door that they are ready and anxious, they gonna feel us, are gonna connect with us. You got to come out there confident, for me it's almost on the borderline of being cocky. All of a sudden you've got that connection—you're *vibing.*"

Wesley said, "This whole game is just based on how *ill* you are, and how *sick* a cat you can be. Sometimes it's about finesse, sometimes we're just on there *spitting*, so we try and be as *raw* as we can be onstage. So you have to rock as hard as you can. We use the word *nasty* for everything."

TREY: We have a saying, *pro nasty,* professionally nasty, that means it's quality—this is not just good, this is the top.

WESLEY: That's our Grade A, that's our professional grade.

TREY: If you want the best and you want the top, you want something from us that's *pro nasty*.

Their lyrics avoid the violence and misogynistic tone of some hip-hop, but the social message is the same, because, they said, it's a portrayal of life: "We're just people that are just talking about what, what's going on, right in front of your eyes, and what people go through on a daily basis, and it's not that hard to relate to it, you know, 'cause a lot of, of America lives this way, you know." Here is a sample of their lyrics from one number performed that night:

What's the difference, at a distance or resistance.
How many times must you hear it before you start to listen,
Before you start the fission of your imagination and your intuition.
'Cause street wisdom don't mean anything for those eh.
Street wisdom don't mean, when there're smarter guys in prison.
'Cause I'm building with men, women and children,
Through the sixth sense, our next level comprehension.
Specifics, but if it's about how loud you play it,
But it past nine, until you're eyes are drumming.
Abuse it 'cause good music is soul soothing as well as mind numbing.
'Cause I'm wondering if my kind's weird for asking this here.
Or spiritually and physically you're just afraid to feel.
And when asked to lend an ear, most people laugh in fear,
Mentally ill prepared to try to see what's really there, or is he scared?

Wesley said, "To give hip-hop its own credit, it's a very powerful media. The words are spoken to you. Storytelling is a huge aspect of hip-hop, so, when you have these vivid stories going on by extremely articulate people, they can reach anybody."

H. Samy Alim, a linguist at Duke University, has studied what he calls Hip Hop Nation Language. He says that hip-hop guards its "street-conscious" identity, using "slang" to connect with African Americans but standard English grammar to appeal to the white audience: "Many hip hop artists know that white suburban fans are attracted to those artists that maintain a core Black urban audience. In a sense many whites play 'cultural catch-up,' letting the Black masses dictate what is in vogue and authentic." He says that the more attention hip-hop artists pay to their speech, the more nonstandard it becomes, raising an interesting question: "Can the conscious use of these forms in the hip hop and the society as a whole, contribute to the continued 'Afro-Americanization' of African American Language," making it "more and more distinct from other varieties of English?"

One aspect of the hip-hop phenomenon that now resonates across the culture is its cross-racial appeal. The TV comedy series *Whoopi*, developed by actress Whoopi Goldberg, features a young white woman acting blacker than her black boyfriend. Commenting on the show, the *New York Times* said that hip-hop has "turned the hilarious improbability of white people who experiment with blackness into a perfectly familiar everyday fact of American life."

Whoopi Goldberg herself said that such racial elision is increasingly the norm in American youth culture: "Eminem is a viable strong male character, who is white *and* black. There's no right or wrong of it, no judgment of it, but it's what's happening in our culture."

The cross-racial appeal was apparent on a rainy day on Sixth Avenue in Manhattan in a store called Fat Beats. Walking up a narrow flight of stairs, we could hear the characteristic scratch, beat, and pulse of the hip-hop music. Fat Beats is not a place to bring people who fear for the future of American English. The record labels don't merely celebrate nonstandard English, they exult in misuse and misspelling, as if it's *cool* to show that you have learned nothing at school. Some might see this as a cult of illiteracy.

Flipping through the record stacks, we found MCs and hip-hop crews with names like Mobb Deep, Ludacris, Rah Digga, Geto Boys, Outkast, and, of course, Snoop Dogg. The titles of their tracks include "So Now UA Mc?," "Enta da Stage," "What U Waitin'," "Who You Wit," "Paid tha Cost to Be da Bo$$," and "Baby aka da #1 Stunna."

This kind of talk is not confined to inner-city ghettos. A whole generation of young, white, and suburban American males is in thrall to the macho swagger of black rappers and MCs. There is even a word to describe them: *wiggers* (for white *niggers*). That word made many wince when it first surfaced in the 1980s. Since 2001, *wigger* has made it into the *New Oxford American Dictionary*.

It was striking how many of the customers were middle-class white teenage boys out to add to their collection of hip-hop and rap music. We listened to these teenagers talking, as they flipped through the once-obsolete vinyl LPs the genre has made essential again. The following is a sample culled from fifteen minutes of conversation between two young men aged about eighteen in June 2003. Caps reversed and baggy pants slung low on their hips, they began by talking about the music.

"The beat is hot. The beat is like shit. And the ladies love it, man."

"What about P. Diddy?"

"Oh yes, he's the man. He's such an ill rapper. . . . Death Jerks, yes, when I was really into underground, I did see him live. He's ill. His freestyle is mad. . . . They had mad beef, there was mad beef between them. . . . When they first, like, both came out of it, it was like they were both like very raw sort. He was half something ill or half—whatever."

Still flipping through the record stacks, they went on to talk about the young women they were meeting at parties.

"Were there bitches at the party?"

"Yeah, there were a couple."

"For real?"

"Sure, man. There've been more ho's recently. I've noticed at underground events. Thank goodness for us, man."

Hip-hop and rap have given new currency to words like *whore* (*ho*) and *bitch*. Cecilia Cutler is a linguist who has studied the appeal of hip-hop for "white male teenagers who are in the process of forming their identities as young men." She believes that the kind of masculinity portrayed is especially appealing: "The urban black male represents someone who knows how to pick up women, who knows how to handle himself on the street, who perhaps knows how to handle a weapon and can take care of himself, and so for the white suburban male these kinds of symbols, this kind of way of walking or talking or dressing, can give one the trappings of a masculinity that doesn't perhaps exist in the safe white suburbs."

Does it appeal to adolescent boys because it comes at a time when a young male is most insecure about his own masculinity? "And the fear of women itself," Cutler said, "where, you know, in rap music there is quite a bit of misogynistic rhyming going on amongst some of the hard-core. That may appeal to young men who are sort of afraid of women or young women and are in the process of trying to figure out how it is that one deals with them."

To call them *bitches* and *ho's* is a way of getting rid of the problem?

Cutler: "Or putting away one's fear of those individuals."

Whatever the psychological motivation, the craze has shoveled a lot of urban black street talk into Mainstream American. Cecilia Cutler gives some examples: "Well, everybody has heard of *She got game* or *He got game,* to mean someone who can play basketball effectively. We have terms like *mad* as a quantifier, so you can say, *It's mad real,* or *It's mad raining.* There are terms like *It's my bad,* to mean, Oh, I just made a mistake, or more colorful *bling bling,* to refer to expensive, gaudy jewelry, but can be applied to any other kind of noun. You could say, *Wassup?* to ask how somebody is, or the term *phat,* which has very positive connotations."

Just after that conversation, we heard a golf commentator on television saying, "That's my bad," about a mistake he had made. We were told of a young African American woman who asked in a jewelry store, "You got any *bling bling* for my *grid*?"—meaning a jewel she could attach to her teeth.

These things move so quickly though the culture that, by November 2003, William Safire noted that *bling bling* for a *glitzy* look in clothing had already moved into the fashion trade and out again, as had the term *ghetto fabulous.* Both were now *history,* because the fashion trend toward ostentation had passed. BG, a rap artist with the group Cash Money Millionaires, apparently coined *bling bling* in the late 1990s. According to Safire, he told MTV News, "But I knew it was serious when I was amazed to see the two words written in diamonds on the NBA championship ring for the Los Angeles Lakers."

The influence of Black English and hip-hop expressions is obvious in another novelty that is driving language change, IM-ing or Instant Messaging. We watched and listened to two fourteen-year-olds, Tom Keller and Kate Stoeckle, IM-ing in a cybercafé in midtown Manhattan, rapidly typing, as they do hours a day after school. Besides the fun of using as many abbreviations as possible—LOL for "laugh out loud," OMG for "Oh my God!" and G2G for "got to go," their IM-ing language is full of words like *Wassup* or *Sup* for "What's up with you?"; *Ima* for "I'm going"; and *Just chillin', dis weekend, I'm doin', You betta call me, Call on ma cell*—phonetic spellings of pronunciations that resemble Black English. It is certainly possible that, just as hip-hop is influencing the way we speak, IM-ing and e-mailing are beginning to alter the way we write.

Baz Dreisinger, who teaches at Queens College, New York, speaks of "a new racial frontier that shaped American culture and especially American music—the frontier that optimists call racial hybridity and pessimists call cultural theft."

How far it is shaping American language remains to be seen. In his book *Doing Our Own Thing*, John McWhorter of Stanford University writes of Black English, "Ebonics has a symbolic meaning to blacks and to the increasing number of non-blacks who incorporate it into their verbal tool kit these days. That meaning is down with the people, real: Black English is today the language of protest par excellence—language from below."

But McWhorter worries that it is moving us further from the norms of written language: "As wonderful as this evidence is that we are truly getting past race, it also means that increasing numbers of Americans are taking as a badge of authenticity a speech style that, with all of its marvels, is very much a spoken one. Ebonics is increasingly a lingua franca among Latino and some Asian teens as well as black ones, for example. More and more we associate genuineness, honesty, and warmth with a kind of English that falls further from the written pole than white-bread spoken English does."

The interesting paradox remains for the nation. African Americans have made huge strides in this society, climbing to the top in every profession, and at the level of popular culture, creating a revolution. Yet for millions of black Americans the language that is so much the expression of that revolution still works to block access to the American Dream.

That is not true for one group that is leading a remarkable turnaround. Millions of black Americans are leaving the North to move back to the South their parents and grandparents fled. Warmer climate, better race relations, and rising prosperity in the region are magnets, but so is a sense of coming "home," and of a stronger black social solidarity. This reverse migration began in the 1970s but accelerated in the next two decades. The black population of the South grew by 1.9 million people between 1970 and 1980, by 1.7 million in the 1980s, and by 3.5 million in the 1990s—in total, already more than left the South from 1914 to 1970. Many of these migrants are well educated and skilled: 30 percent professionals and managers, 19 percent with college degrees. Most of them have settled in middle-class black suburbs around big cities—Atlanta and Orlando the most popular. This phenomenon is so recent that linguists don't know how it will affect Black English—or white English in the South.

seven

Language from a State of Change

The evening we arrived in Los Angeles, we ran into a roadblock on Wilshire Boulevard, with many police cars and news cameras, and several helicopters buzzing overhead. In any other city it might have been a crime scene, a bad traffic accident, or even a terrorist incident, but it was just L.A.'s way of dealing with the Golden Globe Awards, one of Hollywood's big nights. The police were shepherding the swarm of star-bearing limousines each jockeying for the best tactical arrival moment, since even the choreographed posturings on the red carpet are now covered live on television. The movie industry today is more heavily promoted than ever, in mutual complicity with TV, once Hollywood's near-death experience but now its biggest fan club. Sleeping with the enemy being more profitable than competing, the two industries are now embedded in elaborate cross-ownership, production, and distribution alliances. More TV channels need more movies to feed the acres of empty hours, and more television programs make movie news, gossip, fashion a prime commodity. Hollywood called people panting to associate with film actors *starfuckers*. Today, from network morning shows to supper-time tabloids, TV's *starfucking* is as great as that of magazines and newspapers.

Starfucking is just one example of how movie-industry jargon has permeated Mainstream American English. We may never have been near a *studio lot*, but we all know how to talk, literally and figuratively, of *stars, megastars, zoom-ins, cutting to the chase, dissolves,* and *director's cut*. With production in the music industry, television, and movies all centered in Los Angeles, the California voice has a global reach.

America is more movie-obsessed today than at any time since the big-studio days, when the moguls who created Hollywood manufactured personas and fictitious personal lives for their stars and fed them to an astounded world. With movies now being distributed digitally, and revenues from home viewing exceeding theater screenings, the appetite only grows. Hollywood's excesses may be repeatedly trashed in bitter exposés, and the tawdry quality of many movies dismissed by critics, but the people love the product, and the dream factory keeps humming.

No one is quite sure where the name California came from, but the default theory is a Spanish novel about an island with the qualities of paradise. In other words, a fictional paradise, a paradise as an act of imagination. And that fits, because the state of California has been as much the product of imagination as of reality, and Hollywood is only the most visible industry in such an enterprise. From the literal gold rush of 1848 to the end of the twentieth century, California lured generations of dream-seekers, offering new lives, new lifestyles, a more forgiving climate, a less disciplined social structure, and a sense of living in the future. And in time, as they invented their new lives, language became part of the self-invention.

Many observers, and Californians themselves, saw their nation-state as the proto-America of the future—or as writer Diane Johnson put it, "The evolution and fate of California will anticipate those of the rest of America." If that is at all true, California usage will anticipate the fate of American language.

From the beginning, the paradisiacal image of California lured the hopeful to the golden West, from the pioneer settlers who endured the horrors of the wagon trail to Chinese workers (once called *coolies*) and Irish laborers during the railroad building of the 1860s, to the Oklahoma dust-bowl refugees immortalized in Steinbeck's *The Grapes of Wrath*, to blue-collar workers pouring into the aerospace and defense industries of World War II and the Cold War, to blacks escaping the segregationist South, to Mexicans willing to pick the crops of agribusiness, to youths yearning for the lives glimpsed in movies with Natalie Wood and James Dean.

San Francisco was where Sal Paradise, the hero of Jack Kerouac's novel *On the Road*, repeatedly gravitated in his hitchhiking journeys across the country. There Kerouac joined the poet Allen Ginsberg and others in the Beat Movement, in alcohol-and-drug-fueled protest against the conformity and crass consumerism of 1950s America, which made them feel *beaten*, longing for the *beatitude*, or blessedness, of the natural world. The so-called *beatniks* were the first to use *weird* as a term of approbation. Their writings gave American literature a new style, scorning the constrictions of conventional writing—in Kerouac's words, an "undisturbed flow from the mind of personal secret idea-words, blowing (as per jazz musician) . . . limitless blow-on-subject seas of thought, swimming in sea of English with no discipline other than rhythms of rhetorical exhalation." That had a certain California ring to it.

From the 1950s to the 1980s, California seemed so obsessively America's destination that some saw the nation tilted to the west. Megahit songs like "California Dreamin'" ("I'd be safe and warm / If I was in LA / California dreamin' / On such a winter's day") lodged in a generation's collective memory, nourishing a national intuition that California was a paradise of perpetual summer and a *laid-back* attitude toward life.

And always promoting this, lending imagery to the dream, was Hollywood. Its early developers were, of course, immigrants themselves, who started putting their talents on celluloid back east (*back east* is an expression that seems to have died, although *out west* still lives) but came west for ampler space and sunshine. Many of these early moguls spoke idiosyncratic English. But they brought—often from experience in Yiddish theater and vaudeville—a genius for the cultural common denominator that captivated the American public. The advent of the talkies meant that the movies had to settle on a form of English that would be understood and accepted all over the United States. The language they employed at first was more or less the same British-oriented speech common in the theater and in the new medium of radio. Some stars, such as Cary Grant and Katharine Hepburn, clung to it with enduring success even after that accent lost its prestige, but soon more American-sounding actors, such as John Wayne and Gary Cooper, dominated the screens. Their accent, the standard Hollywood accent with its Midwestern origins, was the speech that went around the world after World War II and became in effect the voice of Americanism.

California speech illustrates the way people "middle" their accents. When people with different patterns of speech try to communicate with each other, both sides of the conversation quite unconsciously shift their accent toward the middle. The first people to move to California spoke in a mélange of foreign and American accents. As it began to grow at the beginning of the twentieth century, Los Angeles attracted some Mexicans, Japanese, Russians, and New Yorkers, but principally Anglo-Saxon farmers from the Midwest. So it is not surprising that a Midwestern accent would initially prevail in California. Both Presidents Richard Nixon and Ronald Reagan spoke with that accent—Nixon from birth in California, Reagan a transplant from Midwestern Illinois.

However, language has another tendency. The longer a group of people settle in one place, the more distinctive their way of speech will become. And that has also been happening in California.

Linguists Penelope Eckert and Norma Mendoza-Denton observe, "It takes time and a community to develop common ways of speaking, and English speakers have not been settled in California long enough to develop the kind of dialect depth that is apparent in the East Coast and the Midwest." But this is changing.

The first clear evidence that a new dialect was evolving came in the 1960s. The beach culture had developed long before the Beach Boys released their first Top 40 hit, "Surfin' Safari," in 1962, and Jan and Dean their "Surf City" in 1963, with their utterly hedonistic message:

> *Yeah, and there's two swingin' honeys for every guy*
> *And all you gotta do is just wink your eye*

These and other songs the Beach Boys Web site now calls "eternal anthems of American youth," and the millions of records they sold helped spread what had been to aficionados not just a sport but a whole way of life, lived on the beach, salt-caked and suntanned, with their own insider vocabulary. Soon young people from middle-class suburbs were coming to the beaches, and this surfer slang worked its way inland.

The first time a distinctive California speech pattern came to national attention was when "Valley Girl" became a hit song. *Valspeak,* or the talk of Valley Girls, was made famous by the 1981 song performed by Moon Unit, the fourteen-year-old daughter of Frank Zappa, the bandleader and guitarist known as "the man who put the sneer into rock." The song sneers at the vacuous life of a *val,* a middle-class teenager haunting the Galleria Mall—the latest word in consumer chic—in the Sherman Oaks section of the San Fernando Valley.

> *Fer sure, fer sure*
> *She's a Valley Girl*
> *In a clothing store . . .*
> *Like, OH MY GOD! (Valley Girl)*

Like—TOTALLY (Valley Girl)
Encino is like SO BITCHEN (Valley Girl)
There's like the Galleria (Valley Girl)
And like all these like really great shoe stores . . .

Valspeak included expressions such as *it's so bitchen, bag your face, he's like so gross, barf me out, gag me with a spoon, it's so grody, grody to the max, I'm like freaking out totally.* But it also incorporated surfer slang of the 1980s—*it's so awesome, it's like tubular.*

Penelope Eckert believes that "linguistic style is inseparable from clothing style, hairstyle and lifestyle," and the crux of this stylistic development comes from young people, but especially girls interacting with their peers. Along with William Labov in Philadelphia, she says, "Girls are the movers and shakers in linguistic change. Girls create ways of saying things, advancing changes in the language."

Winnie Holzman is a writer and director acclaimed for her empathy with teenagers in her cult TV series, *My So-Called Life.* She told us that for teenagers, "Your peer group becomes incredibly important to you, your little tribe of friends becomes your new family, and you need to have everything that symbolizes that, everything—the clothes you wear, the way you speak. There's almost nothing more personal than how you express yourself."

Writer-director Amy Heckerling had a different purpose in making another cult classic, her film *Clueless,* starring Alicia Silverstone. Inspired by Jane Austen's novel *Emma,* Heckerling deftly satirized the speech and lifestyle of rich teens in Los Angeles. To research their language, she spent time listening to the students at Beverly Hills High School and watching MTV, finally assembling a *Clueless* dictionary. She said the talk was changing even as they were working on it, "and whenever young actors came in I would always say, What do you say for *good,* for *bad*?"

Their answers fill pages of her dictionary. For *good*, her list includes *coolio, smooth, super, money, nails, tits* (as in *it's the tits*), *feeion* (*fine* broken up into several syllables), *kicking, juice, keen, funky, monster, proper, rad, noble, wicked, tubular, trippy, stoked, rules, rocks, stella, tasty, sweet*. Heckerling dug up an equal variety of ways to say *bad*: *random, heinous, cheesy, blows, bites, bogus, bunk, bum, bum deal, busted, bug, chickenshit, dreaded, drip, the classic, wack, messed, it sucks*, and, of course, *clueless*.

The movie's dialogue was wittier than the mere vocabulary sounds, with a wicked repertoire of put-downs for *nerdy* boys seeking dates—*As if!* or *Not even!* or *Skateboard! That is so five years ago!*—and about clothes—*So last season*, or *I must give her snaps for her total fashion sense*. Ironic flashes of culture were granted these girls, who never seemed to read or know anything but about clothes *in the world of contempo-casual;* hence the ultimate put-down, *She's a full-on Monet, looks good from a distance but a mess close up.*

As we know, linguists believe that movies and television do not change people's language, but the *Clueless* film and the TV series it spawned may be exceptions. In the minds of teenagers a decade later, they seem to have codified some expressions.

We confirmed this by visiting high-school students in Irvine, a new city south of Los Angeles. A generation ago, this was hilly grassland just inland from Newport Beach, part of a vast ranch owned by the Irvine family. Its overnight transformation into a community of a hundred thousand was part of a pattern of insatiable development that dismayed traditional Californians, who saw more and more of their original landscape bulldozed by developers. One of the sweeteners for opponents of this development was the construction of another campus for the expanding University of California. There followed a University High School, and we talked to eight bright students from there, mostly seventeen-year-olds, all white or Asian. The girls told us that *Clueless* had a big impact on them. Here is part of their conversation:

FIRST GIRL: That was like 1997, when I was, like, in fourth grade.

SECOND GIRL: *Clueless.*

FIRST GIRL: Yeah, *Clueless,* 'cause, like, now I'm like permanently, like, messed up because—

SECOND GIRL: Damaged.

THIRD GIRL: —because, like, I say *like, like* and *dude,* every other word because of that movie. It's horrible!

SECOND GIRL: We're not stopping, because that doesn't sound cool anymore.

THIRD GIRL: Like, yes, it does, that is so cool!

FIRST GIRL: I don't know why, it's just, like, it's just stuck, I don't know why.

FOURTH GIRL: When the movie came out, like, even if you just saw the movie once, everybody started saying it, and it became, it became kind of like a cultural trend, sort of. So, like, a lot of kids started saying it, then people would do the "whatever's"

THIRD GIRL: [Doing the hand gestures from the movie] Whatever, moron, get the picture, you're a total loser!

SECOND GIRL: But little kids say that now.

So—the *Clueless* version of California girl talk has already been transmitted half a generation. One of the students wrote in an essay, "Language is born in the youth culture," so, to get a taste of language in gestation, untrammeled by our presence, we arranged for them to have three video minicameras. For four days they taped themselves, hanging out in kitchens and family rooms, driving around, at gatherings of dance and band groups, getting kicked out of a Starbucks for videotaping. The only difference in how they spoke among themselves and to us was that on their own they were freer with four-letter words. We made a list of slang words they used, and at a pizza joint they defined some of them for us, creating a small glossary of teen slang for that place and moment, some of which is probably already out of date. We combined their definitions:

Abe Lincoln. It was so Abe Lincoln—"It's just like the superlative of cool, *it's just Abe Lincoln.*"

Butterface—"You're talking about a girl and everything about her is nice but her face. Also known as *cepterhead.*"

Chills—"Like chilled out, and really laid-back about something, and so they're just *chills* about it."

Dog—"It's not *dog*, it's *dawg*. It means *homie*, it's another word from the rappers. It's not just the word, it's the whole phrase, *Wassup, dawg!*"

Fobby—"It's from *fob*, Fresh Off the Boat. It's, like, the first few years you come and some people will call you a *fob* just because you weren't born here."

It's my ennui—"It's just, yeah, no other way to get around it. It's not the end of everything. That makes it cool."

Gay—"You hear it to describe everything that is stupid, apathetic. It doesn't mean a gay person. It just becomes a word meaning *bad*, and it's, like, this day and age, like we should be past that."

Ghetto—"Like, if you have an old car that's kind of junky and trashy and stuff, you know, it's a *ghetto* car. I catch myself saying, you know, *The beach is so ghetto*, just 'cos it's far away. It's also used to describe people who think they're a *ponce* or whatever, you know, like they try to act like they're gangsters or they're in a gang, and therefore you're cool, he or she thinks *they're so ghetto.*"

Wasian—"White Asian. Acting like ethnicity that they're not, and it doesn't seem like they're doing it well, 'cos they're an *egg*, white outside and yellow inside."

Banana—"Yellow on the outside and white on the inside, so you're Asian on the outside."

Hella—"An American. In San Francisco they say, *It's hella great, hella cool.*"

I got raped—"You did really badly on a test, you *got raped* by the test. Also, it's a sports thing, it's, like, the L.A. Lakers *raped* the Sacramento Kings."

My bitch—"I made that test *my bitch.* It's not being raped, you nailed that test, you aced it, or you did really well. We have this thing with friends, like, sort of, the middle seat in the backseat, it's like *the bitch seat,* like, you know, *you're my bitch,* and we just say *bitch* a lot."

Peeps—"Another rapper word. A friend. *My peeps.*"

Phat—"It's like you're going out dress-shopping with your friends and, like, how do I look in this one? Oh, *you're so phat* in that! It means *cool.* It means *pretty hot and tempting.*"

That's ill—"That means it's good."

Supyo?—"What's up with you?"

Props—"Compliments. You give someone *mad props* and you're, like, this guy wore a kilt to winter formal and you just, like, I respect you, you know, the courage."

Bites—"That means it sucks. Like, *Dude, that has bite,* like, I can't stand this weather, *it like bites,* it's too hot."

Whacked—"Messed up. *Oh, that's whacked,* that's messed up, you shouldn't do that."

Tight (pronounced *tiiight*)—"That's *good. It's tight.* It's like a material possession, like, if you got a new car and it's really nice, you say, *My new car is tight.*"

Über—"It's like super. *Über nerd* is super nerd. You can put *über* in front of anything, it just takes it to an extreme, its *überness.*"

One of the students told us that teens personalize their cell phones down to the core, so why not language? But it's interesting how much they pick up from Black English in personalizing their language. Ten of the twenty-two expressions listed above are borrowed from black talk, or, as a student called it, "the *ghetto fab vernacular* that many teens use today." He also told us, "And teens like informal, *duh!*" *Duh* (meaning, *Don't you get it, stupid?*) was used several times in *My So-Called Life*, as was, for the über-obvious, *duh squared!*

We played back some of our recordings of the Irvine teenagers for Carmen Fought, the linguist who has been studying the emerging California dialect. She said that the speech that is stereotyped in *Clueless* is based on the actual California dialect, which can now be studied as one could study a Southern dialect or a dialect spoken in Appalachia. She said, "It includes some shifts in the sound system. One of the things I've studied is oo-fronting. Words that have 'oo' in them in California English are often pronounced very close to the front of the mouth. So the word *do* might be pronounced more like *dew*. And also words like *go*, *gao*." As we have already noted, linguist William Labov sees this vowel-fronting as a national trend.

Accents in northern California were studied by a team of linguists led by Leanne Hinton at the University of California at Berkeley. They found more examples of back-of-the-mouth vowels moving forward, so that the vowels in *dude* or *spoon* sound like those in *you* or *cute*. The words *boat* and *loan* are pronounced like *bewt* and *lewn*. These linguists also found some chain-shifting of vowels resembling William Labov's Northern Cities Shift around the Great Lakes—*black* sounding like *block*.

Considering the strong influence of the Midwest in originally shaping California speech, it is interesting to compare it today with that of a Midwestern state such as Ohio. Such a comparison is made possible partially by the dialect survey begun by Bert Vaux, a linguistics professor at Harvard, which asks people in different states about a list of words and expressions. By that survey, Ohio and California have a lot in common, with significant majorities saying they pronounced *aunt* as *ant*, *been* as *bin*, and *Mary/merry/marry* all the same. Majorities in both states say *ThanksGIVING*, not *THANKSgiving*, and *CREAM cheese*, not *cream CHEESE*, and think of standing *in line*, not *on line*. But there are differences. Most Californians say they pronounce *cot/caught* the same, but more Ohioans don't. Whereas everybody in both states says *milk shake*, Californians say *soda* for a carbonated drink, Ohioans say *pop*. Californians prefer *firefly* and Ohioans *lightning bug*. One of the sharpest differences came in evaluating the sentence "Pantyhose are so expensive *anymore* that I just try to get a good suntan and forget about it." Californians, by 70 percent, said that was "unacceptable," but 61 percent of Ohioans found it acceptable. Remember that we encountered that usage of *anymore* in the dialect of Pittsburgh. Obviously, *anymore* made it down the Ohio River but not to California.

Carmen Fought grew up in the San Fernando Valley, and the "Valley Girl" song came out when she was in high school. "So I would have to say that my native dialect is Valley Girl English. Even though now I'm a professor and I have this other style that I use in class and in my professional commitments, I can switch to my native dialect when I want to. Sometimes, when I'm trying to explain to the students some point about the California dialect, I will say something like *I totally told him I wasn't gonna do that. And he's all, 'Well, I think you should,'* and it makes a big impact on the students."

She will also say, *Oh my Goh-ud! It was like she-ow ba-a-a-d*, and allow her voice to "go a little creaky" at the end, another California feature.

In speaking these examples, Carmen often raises her inflection at the ends of sentences, yet another sign of the California dialect. She can imagine that in twenty years a governor of California might be saying, *Well, I do have to do some bills that I need to pass in order for us to cut taxes by?* Nor would she be surprised to be on a plane and hear the Californian pilot say, *Like, we're gonna be cruising at fifteen thousand feet?*

"Everyone will hear that and think, That sounds completely un-marked."

Another feature she mentioned was *I'm all* as a quotative, introducing quoted speech—for example, *"So I'm all, 'I don't think I'm gonna go,' and he's all, 'I think you should.' And I'm all, 'Why?' And he's all, ' 'Cause it'll be fun.' And I'm all, 'I don't think so.'* I hear my students often with long strings of these."

She hears all these features spreading more widely throughout California. "You hear it in more places than you used to. I hear newscasters on local TV who to me sound like Valley Girls—you hear those fronted vowels in their English. The sounds that are different in Valley Girl English are the sounds of standard California English now. And you hear the same characteristics of California dialect spreading to other parts of the country. . . . The use of *like* and things like this that may have originated in California but are now spreading. The California dialect is here to stay. It's not just a passing fad."

Men have some of the characteristics associated with Valley Girl talk, but with a quantitative difference. Carmen said that, though male students say *like* and use the rising intonation and the fronted vowels, they generally speak *Surfer Dude,* an observation that, naturally, took us to talk to surfers.

At Surfers Point in Ventura County, we met George Plomarity, a young writer who has had a couple of poems published by the very selective *New Yorker* magazine and had trained as a paralegal. But he lives to surf, and to feed the habit he works at a surfer hangout near the beach in Ventura, the Bad Ass Café. Not only is surfer talk evolving, like every form of specialized slang or jargon, but surfers are as much influenced by other features of the California dialect as Valley Girl talk is by surfers. When we met George working behind the counter, he said there wasn't much business at the café because the surf was too good. "Surf's too good, for sure. For sure." His accent had the vowel-fronting in *for sure,* making it *fer sher.*

In his classic beat-up 1970 Volkswagen minibus, five year older than he is, George took us a few miles up the coast to Rincon Point, one of the three greatest surfing locations in the world. It was late January, but the warm sunshine made it obvious why Californians became such surfing addicts—they can do it all year round. As the point came into view, George said, "Ah, there's a lot of people in the water. Look at that great wave, that guy's still going on it! He's gonna set up for a little barrel on the inside."

In the 1980s, we filmed a punk-rock band called the Surf Punks, and on our laptop now we showed the sequence to George, with the Surf Punks talking 1980s *Surfer Dude*. On the film they said, "Certain words find their way into the whole language and some of it is pretty *off the wall*."

So—check it out, dude. Like I was cruisin' the beach yesterday and the waves were totally crazy and it was really hot.

When the wave comes over your head, it makes like a tube or pocket. So, if you're in the tube, you're taking the highest risk and you're very rad.

I saw this chick and she had a totally tight bod and she was totally buff and that means she's in shape, and she's clean, and she looks good.

I see some dude's wearing some rad outfit and just go, "Wow! That's totally rad, that's pretty gnarly." Look, we're all wearing the same watches. That's totally rad, way rad. Fully rad.

In that dialogue, one can hear terms, like *check it out*, used that same year by the black rappers we filmed in Philadelphia, and some, like *tight*, used today by the high-school students at Irvine, albeit with some change in meaning.

George Plomarity said those words are still current: "Those words are all used and definitely, like, find their way into vernacular speech. You know, you can hear everyone describing things as *rad,* or people being, like, hot or *truly radical*—a lot of those phrases that came out in the early eighties got, got co-opted, you know, they got taken over by like some corporate people that use them to *shlog* T-shirts. *To the max,* that's a wonderful example of something that was taken by Pepsi in the eighties, you know, and just whored until it's not used anymore."

Asked for new surfing expressions, or expressions new to surfers, George said, "*Full on*'s a great example. *Off the wall,* that's another phrase you hear a lot, you know? Or *right on,* or *phat,* meaning something that was really big, that was *phat,* like a *phat air.*" That means going off the wave into the air and being really high up.

Plomarity believes that surfers themselves have moved into the mainstream of the culture, and that's why their expressions are becoming an influence. "We have like a lot of people that are professionals. They'd go out and surf in the morning, you know, get as crazy as they can and really push themselves to their limits, and then take a shower and go to the law office. And they're going to carry over that language with them, you know, and a great example of that would be, like, the phrase *caught inside.* You know, you hear that all over the place, in describing any situation where you suddenly have to try and deal with, with a whole lot of stuff coming at you at the same moment."

Listening to George describe the perfect *ride,* we felt that surf slang remains as vigorous and inventive as ever: "You know, waves break in sections, so you can talk about, like—wow!—you know, that first section was sick, you know, that drop was really heavy, it made that bottom come around, went through that mushy part, and then it just jacked on that second bowl, got that floater, came into the inside, and just cracked that lip as hard as I could, set up for that barrel, and just—right on into the green room—sick."

Surfboarding begat skateboarding, which begat snowboarding, and each new sport begat its own new slang and jargon.

Skateboarding is one of America' fastest-growing sports, and one of the kings is Steve Badillo, co-author of two books on the sport. He's also head instructor at the Skatelab Skatepark at Simi Valley, California, an indoor-outdoor facility of curved ramps and rails where skaters can learn and practice. Since skateboarders consider themselves "urban guerrillas" because they like to go out and skate everything in the street, some cities have banned the sport except in specially created parks. In skaters' minds this has created an us-versus-them mentality with civic authority. Part of the mystique is that skateboarding is the ultimate democratic sport, because poor people can do it in the streets. Steve Badillo explained, "When the skaters are out in public, while you guys see it as a curb, stairs, a handrail, a bank, or a ledge, we look at it as, Is it skateable? Can we bust out on it? When you get into a park and there's a lot of guys skating and everyone's hyping each other on, and everyone's trying to outdo each other, you know that's the time to just really go out and, and, you know, blast the biggest airs you can, and do the longest grinds you can. I have a bag of tricks, so I don't really have any favorites, other than the ones that make me feel good. But I like blasting airs, for sure."

Badillo showed us *blasting airs,* in which he skated up and down steeper and steeper ramps and finally up a vertical wall, to give him the momentum to go airborne, to fly across a wide gap in the wall. Some of Badillo's lingo showed clear borrowing from surfing terms—for example, *regular foot,* for left foot forward, and *goofy foot,* for right foot forward. Other skateboard terms were so far out that he needed to translate almost every other word.

Grinding—riding the wheel trucks on the underside of the board along the edge of a ramp, or along its railing or coping.

Riding the nose—standing at one end of the board to emulate the surfing maneuver.

Ripping, rippers—to describe kids who are just *tearing it up*—out there on the course and having a good time.

Downhill bombing—most skaters love the basic natural form of just going down a hill as fast as you can, carving it up, and having fun with it.

Badillo told us, "In skateboarding one little false move, one little thing off, and you're, you're slamming, you're taking a fall."

Although it claims to have lower injury rates than many sports, skateboarders fall a lot, and Badillo says, "You will bleed, but that's the part of skateboarding that attracts people—the extreme aggression in skating required to overcome the risk is what gives you motivation." Enthusiasm tends to fall off as skaters emerge from their teens. As one of Steve's books, *Skateboarder's Start-Up,* unsentimentally states, "Anyone past 25 usually has reservations. They won't push themselves and attempt the more difficult tricks. It's much easier for little kids to be fearless."

That is not true of snowboarding, which people of all ages have adopted as an alternative to skiing, and which is now accepted as an Olympic sport. From Los Angeles, the city where one can surf and snow-ski on the same day, we drove up to the Big Bear Mountain ski resort, a hundred miles east of the city. That day, more people were snowboarding than skiing. One of the young aces, Jayk Goff, demonstrated some of the most challenging tricks while making comments in the snowboarders' whole new lexicon. *Sticking it clean* means pulling off a trick to perfection. If you can repeat the trick again and again, you've *got it dialed in. Kodak courage* means trying extra hard because your girlfriend or someone is taking your picture. That way you *get more props.* He explained that *props* (another crossover from Black English) came from *showing proper respect,* the opposite of *dis,* or *dissing,* for showing disrespect.

In Jayk's snowboard lingo one can hear echoes of other slang we've heard in California. Jayk said of a particularly hard trick, "That's *sick.*

That's the super, like, *super-sick stuff.* Like, someone goes off and does something and *stomps it clean,* then you're gonna *give him props,* and that's gonna be something *sick.* And that's when you're gonna, like, it's gonna raise the level of riding, and everybody's just gonna, like, just get everybody *amped* up."

For a long time, the most dedicated surfers, skaters, and snowboarders inhabited separate universes. Today, it is increasingly common for someone who surfs to enjoy snowboarding or skateboarding as well. The result is that the three separate slangs are cross-fertilizing one another and their words and phrases are gaining wider currency.

It was not only Jayk's snowboarding vocabulary that we found fascinating. As a twenty-year-old from Redlands, California, he was a virtuoso user of the word *like.* As we've heard, young Californians say *like* where previous generations said *um* or *er,* and they use it, as Carmen Fought pointed out, to mean quote-unquote. Jayk quite unconsciously used *like* thirteen times, in both senses, in the next sixty-nine words: "Yeah, *like,* I, *like,* what I say, *like,* sometimes people just don't understand it, *like,* I, my terminology for certain things, which is, *like, like,* who, my clique, my group, *like* my friends, *like,* nobody else understands it, so if I go someplace new, they are, *like,* they don't know it so, *like,* and they are, *like,* they are, *like,* 'What are you talking about? *Like,* What'd you say?' "

One of our high-school students in Irvine wrote in a paper, "The word *like* has barely any meaning; a placeholder for keeping the space-sound busy when thinking abilities cannot outrun the tongue. Smokers, as I have noted, do not put this word to such heavy use." That's an interesting observation in view of the following anecdote about a Princeton student published in *The New Yorker:* "Her roommate, Jacqui Neiss, talks about using her looks to get what she wants, 'Like last night I'm desperately out of cigarettes, running around, and I'm like, "Hi, random guy, can you give me a cigarette?" ' "

Some of these uses of *like* have spread widely, noted among people a generation older in New York and among teenagers in London.

Stephen Levy, a linguist at Queen Mary University, London, states that popular notions of *like* merely as a "filler or fumble" are inaccurate. Levy analyzed the speech of children aged ten and eleven in an outer-London school and found many different uses of *like*. In one example ("They had to jump *like* a meter away from the actual acid"), *like* appeared to convey the meaning of *approximately*. In another ("They put *like* this bandage stuff around it"), *like* served "to highlight the introduction of new entities into discourse." Another example used *like* (as so commonly in California) as a quotative, introducing reported speech ("When my brother yells, he's *like*, 'Do it now!' *like* that, and I'm *like*, 'No!' ") There, Levy says, *like* is not intended to introduce a literal, verbatim quotation, but an illustrative example, letting her "offer a stereotypical response for her brother." He found *like* also used "to frame a restart where a speaker starts off on a particular track and feels the need to rephrase" ("If you *like*, was *like*, *like* talking too much, he would tell you off"). Levy detects one linguistic role for *like*, similar to *you know*, "to build conversational solidarity and negotiate common ground." He said that girls used it more often than boys, and he found that "compatible with a body of linguistic evidence that in Western cultures women employ a co-operative conversational style more than men."

Valley Girls, Surfer Dudes, skateboarders, and snow punks all illustrate the bigger point that a huge amount of fresh language and new vocabularly is always being created by the young of each generation. But even in a society as youth-obsessed as California's, there are other powerful engines of social change, which lead in turn to further linguistic evolution.

California is far from being a state just of blond surfers and Valley Girls. Most Californians don't live anywhere near the beach. Because there are large communities of Hispanic and African American Californians, as well as Japanese and Chinese, and more recently Koreans and Vietnamese, California is one of the most racially mixed states in the country, and that diversity is bound to affect California English in the long run.

Besides these important ethnic influences, California's leading-edge culture entails a tolerance for gender diversity that has been well ahead of most of America for at least two generations. The entire nation has come a long way since feminism and women's lib became part of the political agenda in the 1960s, and the changes since have transformed perceptions in the workplace. Most companies and institutions now require codes of conduct and declarations against sexual harassment or discrimination.

One interesting institution into which this new sensitivity has taken something of a bite is the U.S. military. Not only are the armed forces required to enlist women as a matter of promoting sexual equality, but women's skills are needed to operate increasingly complex systems in the age of computer-driven warfare. Though sexual-abuse scandals still erupt periodically in the services, the fact that they become public, and that disciplinary action often follows, indicates a new culture in this generation of military leaders. But the U.S. military services have always been a forcing ground for change. They were among the first national institutions to confront racism. In 1948, President Truman ordered the armed forces to offer "equality of treatment and opportunity: regardless of race, color, religion, or national origin." Now they have added sex—but not sexual orientation.

Today, the military services are on the front line of the war on sexism. We visited the U.S. Marine Corps at Camp Pendleton, California, and their Recruiting Depot in San Diego. Women marines receive basic training separately, but here at the tough boot camp, male recruits have respect for women drilled into them as part of basic training. On the firing range at Pendleton, we talked to two drill sergeants, the traditional in-your-face disciplinarians all recruits fear, their eyes just shaded by the brims of their hats. Staff Sergeant Sandy Beavers explained the rules: "There's a green zone, a yellow zone, and a red zone. The green zone would be just a normal interaction between male and female. The yellow zone would probably be the sort of comments where it could be taken as something that may be sexually orientated or may cause someone to feel uncomfortable. The red zone is considered just to be a blatant sexual remark, like *Check him or her out,* or *Look what they have there,* or *I want to get some of that.*"

Marines, like all servicemen, are notorious for their reflexive profanity, from the World War II acronym SNAFU (Situation Normal All Fucked Up) to the time-honored tendency to insert the word *fuck* repeatedly in a sentence, even between syllables of individual words. Has that changed? With a straight face, Staff Sergeant Scott McLaughlin added: "We try to discourage profanity, believe it or not, as much as we can. Just because it projects an unprofessional image."

At San Diego, newly recruited marines were marching in the hot sun, and sounding off the cadence with a drill instructor marching by them, his ceremonial sword flashing on his shoulder. The recruits were dressed in *camies,* camouflage fatigues, whose patterns are now designed by computer, one style for woodland, another for desert. Just off the parade ground, to symbolize the new policy, are the recently erected statues of two drill sergeants, a man and a woman. Near that memorial, we met Staff Sergeant Denise Ruiz, eleven years in the marines, with an appearance that would look good on a recruiting poster. We asked if the new policy had changed how marines talked. She said, "The way the men talk? As far as cursing and telling jokes? It all depends on how you are. If you can tell a joke just as good as they can, laugh, tell yours, too. If you're the type that you don't wanna hear jokes like that, tell them that. And they should respect that. If you'd like it, by all means. If you don't, say something."

The one area where all the services are encouraged not to "say something" touches homosexuality. Bill Clinton politically poisoned the beginning of his presidency by trying to lift the ban against gays in the military. Senior officers dug in their heels, and all Clinton got was a compromise. Staff Sergeant Beavers explained it: "We don't ask, and they don't offer that information up. Basically, the don't-ask, don't-tell policy." And is that working? He said crisply, "I think it is, sir." Advocates of a freer policy say it isn't working, because there is still covert harassment, and discharges for outed homosexuality continue.

Don't ask, don't tell is at the other end of the cultural spectrum from San Francisco, where nobody has needed to ask for a long time because everybody has been telling—everything, embracing in the process a far wider range of gender definition and terminology than when we filmed the gay community in the 1980s. Today, the committee that organizes the internationally famous annual Gay Pride Day and march in San Francisco has expanded its name to the San Francisco Lesbian Gay Bisexual and Transgender Community. We attended a meeting of the committee as they discussed the next march and explained the new terminology.

In the 1980s, we had filmed a stand-up comedian, Tom Ammiano, performing a nightclub routine on the various kinds of *queens,* and it went like this:

> There's dizzy queens and mad queens and lipstick queens and drag queens and macho queens and feather queens and disco queens and leather queens and tragic queens and magic queens and screaming queens and dreaming queens and attitude queens and platitude queens and hustle queens and muscle queens and pissy queens and sissy queens, black queens, white queens, left queens, right queens, red queens, dead queens, acid queens, speed queens, down queens, and weed

queens, Wizard of Oz'd queens and closet queens, size queens
and aging queens and raging queens.

Ammiano ran for mayor of San Francisco in 2003, saying he could
save the taxpayers money by being both mayor and his own first lady.
San Franciscans were amused but voted for someone else.

Today, the Lesbian Gay Bisexual and Transgender Parade committee told us, they could think of still other kinds of *queens,* but the
word was too narrow a focus for the community (*queens* being only
gay men), because many other people now had a voice, and because
the idea of gender had increasingly become "malleable and fluid."
One woman said, "I'm very proud to be part of the gay, bisexual,
lesbian group," but she wouldn't want to be called a *queen,* " 'cause I
identify as a female, and for someone to call me a *queen* . . . is very
derogatory." Out of this new diversity has sprung a lexicon of new
terms:

Transgender—An umbrella term to encompass many forms of behav-
ior, including *transsexuals, transvestites, drag queens, drag kings, cross-dressers, female illusionists, gender benders, gender queens*—although not limited to those
definitions, and not all of those people want to be called *transgender.* The
major purpose was to obtain civil-rights and human-rights protection
that had previously been granted to other groups. The result in San
Francisco was a transgender protection ordinance. *Tranny* is a nickname
for someone showing the potential to be *transgender,* not to be confused
with *tranny,* car buffs' slang for "transmission."

Transsexual—Originally defined as people who had undergone hor-
monal or surgical intervention to make a physical transition from one
gender to another, but now applied more vaguely.

Pansexual—Devised to cover a wider definition than *bisexual*—for example, a man or woman loving a *transgender* person.

Intersexual—A term adopted for people born with genitalia neither male nor female, as part of a movement to prevent surgical alteration to a gender arbitrarily decided by a doctor.

Two-spirit—Traditionally used by Native American communities to describe people who weren't apparently male or female but a third, or a *two-spirit* person.

One term that interested these people was *San Francisco Democrat*, which they said was Republican Party code for *gay*, and applied to liberal Democrats whether from Hawaii or Massachusetts.

Another expression gaining currency is *metrosexual*, especially popular in Honolulu, denoting heterosexual men obsessed with such grooming activities as facials, manicures, and body-hair waxing, the latter now known as *manscaping*.

California culture, at least the San Francisco end of it, often runs a little fast for the rest of the country. In 2004, the new mayor, Gavin Newsom, not gay himself, suddenly began issuing marriage licenses for gays. That touched off a huge debate nationally, provoking President George W. Bush to propose a constitutional amendment to save civilization by defining marriage as between a man and a woman.

In 1993, PBS showed a season of the TV series based on *Tales of the City*, by San Francisco writer Armistead Maupin. One theme was a love affair between a man and a character played by Olympia Dukakis who was transsexual, a man living as a woman. It attracted some of the highest ratings ever for public television, but some stations complained that the content was too adult. PBS dropped the series, which was later picked up by the cable channel Showtime.

With the San Francisco LGBT committee, we noted the increasing use of *queer* (hitherto usually an insult, an expression of homophobia) by the gay community itself. In fact, the theme for their parade in 1993 was "The Year of the Queer." Former mayoral candidate Tom Ammiano, a Democrat, jokes that his gay Republican friends used to cheer, "We're here, we're queer, we're sorry!" By 2000, they had adopted *queerific*, to suggest that being *queer* was *terrific*.

We asked one of the committee members, Calvin Gibson, who is African American, whether using *queer* themselves was analogous to blacks' using *nigger* but being offended if white people did. He said, "That's exactly what it's like. I believe it's because people feel disempowered and this is one way to empower themselves. If we can use the word *queer* so many times that it just becomes a normal word in our language without any consequences, then I think we see ourselves as being more empowered. So—it sort of proves the point that you can change the meaning of words."

In fact, in recent years the word *queer* has lost some of its homophobic sting in the general culture. Noting the number of movies and television shows embracing gay themes, *USA Today* said 2004 was "the Year of the Queer in Hollywood." This is a telling example of how rapidly words can change their meaning or lose their capacity to wound.

Linguist Dennis Baron has studied the gender issue in language and says that feminism has also had its impact on which words women choose to use or not to use. Between the 1970s and 1990s, *girl* was taboo. A *Doonesbury* comic strip in the 1970s had a proud father showing off a newborn daughter and saying, "It's a baby woman!" Now *girl* is back in favor with the advent of *girl power,* perhaps also because it has wide currency among black women. Women have taken a term that had a negative connotation and made it positive. He thinks one reason for the change is that the women's movement has progressed to more important issues like economics and is willing to let the semantic issues find a place that is comfortable for the women who are using the terms.

He says that *guy* is an interesting example. Though it is a masculine term in the singular, which some feminists still won't use, most people now think that *guys* is not particularly masculine. His college-age daughter says it is perfectly okay for all-female groups to be *guys.* "We can be *guys,* we can be *dudes,* we can be *bitches*—whatever!" The nice thing about this, Baron says, is that "people get a sense that they can empower themselves to use whatever language they want. That's the positive effect of political correctness. People can say, 'I've got a right to call myself what I want.' "

That idea reminded us of something Carmen Fought said about the California dialect. The original settlers brought their dialects from other parts of the country. "And then, as younger generations of Californians have grown up, they want to have their own way of talking. They need to have a way to identify themselves as 'I'm from California.' For all of us, language is so tied up with our identity. We want to sound like people we want to be like."

That raises interesting questions. Does the spread of California dialectical features across America—"oo" fronting, rising inflections, use of *like* and *all* as quotatives—mean that young people in the rest of the country yearn to be like Californians? Is the magic draw still strong enough to make them want to emulate that culture? Or is this a cultural lag, something left over from songs and images of the past?

Carmen Fought raised a feature that especially puzzles us—the habit of rising inflections—or *uptalk*, as some linguists call it. It was a question that disturbed Molly Ivins, the writer in Austin, Texas: "What I find very troubling is the spreading of this sort of Valley Girl intonation, where every statement ends in a question, so that everything a woman says sounds as though she's not really sure of it. It's that continual question mark, as though to assert yourself and, so, okay, state something is either factually correct or something that you believe were too assertive for a woman, that it would be unfeminine."

But we hear the rising inflection also being used by some men, although more commonly by women, and spreading across the country. What does it mean? Does it indicate some unconscious uncertainty lurking in the psyches of young Californians and young Americans elsewhere? Does changing language mean a changing American consciousness? And what does that mean for the future of the country, not just the language?

Or is the rising inflection as innocent as a wish to connect with a listener, a way of saying, in effect, *Are you following me?* In other words, might it be simply a wish to please—not an unfamiliar trait in the American personality?

As young Californians say, *Whatever!* It is hard to resist the conclusion that California English is becoming one of the most influential dialects, not only in the United States but throughout the English-speaking world.

eight

Teaching Computers to Speak American

The face on the computer screen is robotic. It is an electronic graphic, digitally composed, a fusion of Caucasian, Hispanic, and Asian features. From time to time the head tilts and the eyes blink convincingly. But when it speaks its voice is flat and unemotional. We hit the computer keyboard and it talks: "My name is Baldy. Welcome to the Stanford Lab."

We are at Stanford University, where several of the scholars we have cited are based, on one of the most beautiful campuses in America. You approach it from Palo Alto, an hour south of San Francisco, along a mile-long drive lined with royal palms, the tiled roofs of the Mission-style architecture set against a backdrop of mountains. The main quad was designed by Frederick Law Olmsted, the creator of New York's Central Park. We came to talk first with Clifford Nass, professor and director of the Institute for Communication Research. Nass is an intense and lively man with an eagerness for his subject that is infectious. He has been praised by Bill Gates, chairman of Microsoft, who said Nass had shown them "some amazing things."

Nass is working at one of the cutting edges of computer research—how to teach computers to speak to us and understand us, and thus be easier to use. The ability to speak and understand language almost defines what it is to be human, so Nass's work raises fundamental questions about the future of American speech and about language itself. We talked to him in a shady spot off the main quad.

Our brain, Nass says, is built to generate and to understand speech. Even people with IQs as low as fifty and brains as small as four hundred grams, less than a third the size of a normal human brain, can fully speak. And on the understanding side, children one day old can distinguish speech from any other sounds, and by four days old they can distinguish their own language from other languages. Starting at eighteen months, they can learn two words every day on average, "a remarkable built-in capacity."

More than anything else, says Nass, human beings, when they grow up, are voice-activated: "The minute they hear anything that sounds even in the most remote way like human speech, they'll respond to it as though they are dealing with a human. So they'll bring to bear not only understanding the words, but looking for what we call paralinguistic cues, things like, What is the gender of the voice? What is its personality, its emotion, et cetra? And even though they won't be aware they are doing it, and in fact will deny that they're doing it, nonetheless, because they are built to do it, they are voice-activated: they automatically do it. And they will react as they would if they were interacting with real people."

Whatever stereotypes people bring to bear in hearing a human talk will come into play when they are dealing with a computer: "If the computer has a female voice, it will be perceived as doing stereotypically better in areas that are typically associated with women—for example, discussion of love and relationships. It will be perceived as being a worse teacher of technical subjects like physics."

In one experiment, a voice-based computer tutored people in three subjects—love and relationships, mass media, and engineering. A different computer, with a different voice, then praised the performance of the tutoring computer. Both computers used human voices that were either male or female. Consistent with the stereotype that praise from males is taken more seriously than praise from females, participants in the experiments rated the tutor computer as significantly more competent and more friendly when it was praised by a "male" computer than by a "female" computer. "We were stunned and disturbed by these results," Nass says. They thought to solve it by substituting synthetic voices so clearly nonhuman that people would not succumb to gender stereotypes, but people still did.

Nass has done a series of experiments involving politeness. "It's rather silly to worry about being polite to a computer," he says, "but people are." We mentioned the joke that Canadians are so polite they say thank you to the ATM. Nass said, "It's highly natural, and it's probably much harder to avoid saying it than to say it." In the experiments, when a computer asked people what they thought about it, the respondents thought that computer was nicer than one that didn't ask. "They'll say it was more intelligent, more likable, more enjoyable. Even though, when you ask them afterwards, 'Were you trying to be polite?' They say, 'Of course not, it's ludicrous to be polite to a computer!' "

People were also, as Nass put it, "suckers for flattery." In one study experimenters gave them feedback, reporting how well or poorly they did on a task. When people received a positive comment, whether they thought it was accurate or simply flattery, they liked the computers more and had a great time. They also rejected what they considered false criticism.

Nass showed us up to his cramped and slightly chaotic office and then down the hall to his lab. The lab is a poky place packed with video recorders, projection screens, computers, and a veritable spaghetti of computer cables. It is in this wired-up jumble that Nass's research really comes to life.

There are three different aspects to this research: how to make computers understand us, how to make them talk so that we understand them, and how we feel about interacting with them. The last is the subject of a book Cliff Nass co-authored on how people react with computers. He and Byron Reeves say that we are conditioned by our evolution to treat things that act socially as if they were actually social, that we bring "old brains" to modern media: "Absent a significant warning that we've been fooled, our old brains hold sway and we accept media as real people and places."

Nass believes that in three to five years synthetic speech will be indistinguishable from human speech. What makes this simulation possible is the ability computers offer to break down the way we talk into small pieces of sound, to put them in a context—actually, in hundreds of contexts. Human speech can thus be built up artificially. This has already been achieved, to a sophisticated, if not yet perfect, level.

Cliff Nass showed us his work with the computer-generated image named Baldy, developed through Veepers technology by Don Mesaro of the University of California at Santa Cruz. Baldy will say whatever he's told to say through words typed on a computer keyboard. When Nass types, "My name is Baldy, welcome to the Stanford Lab," Baldy says it. If Nass trips on the keyboard, as he did, and types "t-t-o to the Stanford Lab," Baldy will speak it as typed, appearing to stutter over the "t-t-o," his lips moving in synchronization with the words. What is missing from his speech is personality. Nass says that "the only hard part is recognizing emotion." To our ears, this absence of expression was the most unnatural thing about Baldy's speech. One wants to say to Baldy, "Do it again but with more feeling!" We had to remember, however, that this was speech not assembled from words previously recorded by a real person but synthesized from artificial components.

At this rate of progress, Nass said, we might soon reach a point at which a computer-generated person could read the news on television, like the character Max Headroom in a British movie. We resisted the temptation to observe that, watching some television, one might think this had already happened.

Using Baldy, Nass and his colleagues have discovered many interesting things about how people react to computers. Among their findings is that Baldy is easy to understand, even for nonnative speakers of English. When people are confronted with a synthetic face like Baldy's and a synthetic voice, they are very accepting and comfortable with it.

The applications are potentially enormous, particularly looking ahead a few years to the time when the kinks are removed and more expression can be added to future Baldys. Nass believes, for instance, that a time could come when a Baldy could read aloud all the books in the Stanford Library, or any books anywhere, to people who couldn't read for themselves, or who needed their eyes for another task. All that would be needed would be to scan those books digitally and feed the scanned file to Baldy. Theoretically, that could be done in any language, or in any accent or regional dialect of a language.

The technology also has applications in education, in which individuals could be taught in a more focused way, with better understanding. Nass says, "When [the voice is] coupled with a face that matches, we know people will pay more attention, learn more, understand better." He said it could be used for voting, because the blind or illiterate now have to have someone with them, which means they cannot vote secretly. With this technology, the ballot could be read to them. But the Nass research also brings interesting complications to the surface. Since it turns out that people respond similarly to computer-simulated faces and real people, they react negatively when their expectations are crossed. For example, the researchers deliberately substituted a real human voice recording for Baldy's computer-simulated speech. Baldy still moves his lips and eyes as before, but respondents view him with feelings of suspicion. The combination is seen as less trustworthy, less intelligent, less reliable. The same is true when they use a real human face and match it with a synthetic voice. Even though people in general like a human voice better than synthetic one, when it's paired with an artificial face, like Baldy's, it triggers feelings of suspicion and worry. Respondents trust both mismatches less than the voice/face combinations when both are real or both are synthetic.

Nass says, "When humans see faces and voices, they integrate them. They can't listen separately." He demonstrated this with another experiment, using a still photograph that can be animated by computer to move lips and blink when it talks, as they feed it different voices. For example, they used a photograph of Robert MacNeil, with his voice saying the sentence "Would you hire me for a job requiring contact with the public?" Nass said that was credible, because the voice fitted the face of a Caucasian speaking standard American English. Then he showed MacNeil's face speaking the same sentence but with the voice of John Baugh, the linguist we had encountered earlier, also a Stanford professor. Nass said, "Now, stereotypically, that voice is appropriate, it's a Southern accent." Then he repeated the sequence, keeping John Baugh's voice but this time also the face of Baugh, who is African American. What had sounded like a white man talking Southern now "sounded" stereotypically African American. "Our brains automatically integrate the face and the voice and come up with the single viewpoint," Nass said.

So, we asked, will this new technology reinforce these stereotypes, that a black man and a white should each speak in a certain way, or could it be used to break them down, in the interest of promoting greater tolerance for diversity? It could do either, Nass said, depending on the motivation and the incentives. If you simply paired stereotypical faces and accents, that would reinforce stereotypes. The technology permits mixing and matching, but, as we have seen, the psychological tendency is to distrust a mismatch. "And that wouldn't just apply to

African Americans, that would apply to any ethnicities," Nass said. "People, when they see a face, they bring to bear stereotypes about how that person should behave, think, and speak. When those stereotypes run counter, people don't say, 'Oh, this person was brought up in a particular place, that's how their family spoke,' they say, 'There's something wrong here.' And that mistrust has consequences."

"Even obvious synthetic speech, like Baldy's," Nass said, "will be assigned a gender, will be assigned an emotion, an accent, a location in the country, a personality—the entire range of things that we do when we hear a human voice. So, if there is a synthetic female voice, or a real female voice from a computer, that computer is now a female, from Alabama, with all the stereotypes that we would associate with an actual human female from Alabama."

What would determine whether the technology reinforces or modifies these stereotypes? "Well, if we started out with the naïve approach, which was, if this regional accent is stereotyped as being unintelligent, let's make sure we never use it in any application that would imply a need for intelligence, then those stereotypes would be strong reinforced. And because of the ubiquity of computer systems, it would make those stereotypes even stronger. If we said, 'Let's do the opposite'—let's say, 'Whenever we need a really intelligent application, let's not search for a regional accent that's marked as intelligent, let's find one and just have all the content that requires intelligence delivered by that accent. Like having all the physics lectures done in that regional accent'—that would then, because of the way our brains are voice-activated, that would lead us to weaken that stereotype and potentially eliminate it."

Or, we suggested, thinking of Jeff Foxworthy, have all brain-surgery instruction done with a Southern accent? Over time, Nass said, that would lead us to believe that brain surgeons could be, or *should* be, Southern.

We left the lab to walk around to the Education Department, where

John Baugh works, to ask what he thought of the Nass experiments and stereotyping. He said many people assume that, because we have television and radio and we're all hearing the same voices time and again through broadcasters, somehow our stereotypes have diminished. "But his work demonstrates that there are clear correspondences between individuals, how they look, and preconceptions about how they should sound." In other words, strangers meeting Baugh might think he should be speaking African American Vernacular, which he did as a child.

If this technology were in the hands of a government agency, with the promotion of racial equality an important policy goal, it would probably make an effort to use the technology to break down stereotypes. Baugh thinks commercial ventures will focus primarily on marketability, and so are likely to adopt the technology to home in on markets they seek to target: "We see this a little bit on radio right now, so that various radio stations are tailored to particular markets. The African American markets clearly use DJs that are geared towards the African American market."

Cliff Nass introduced us to one practical application of his research. He was retained by BMW to consult on the choice of voice appropriate for the speech-recognition system in one of its latest models. Like those in other luxury cars, the system is designed to let the driver place phone calls, tune his radio, record memos, and operate a satellite navigation system without taking his hands from the wheel. We drove around trying out the system as Nass described the process the automaker had gone through. Consumer surveys show that the typical purchaser of BMW's high-end luxury sedan is a high-earning, successful alpha male, the kind of man who doesn't like being told what to do by anyone, let alone a woman. Initially the voice designed for the car was female, and German drivers were very upset. We wondered, only a little facetiously, whether American men weren't used to having females tell them how to drive. Nass said, "I think so, but I don't know that they'd pay extra for it."

BMW had to recall the product and change the voice to male, which is where Cliff Nass came in, to decide what kind of male voice—and here a forest of stereotypes sprang up. They focused first on what relationship BMW wanted between car and driver: the car being in control, the car as having a chauffeur, the car as your best friend. They decided the best model was a copilot, so that the driver was in charge (because BMW drivers like to feel they are in control of the car), but they also wanted to create the sense that if the driver got distracted or something happened, the car would be forgiving. If the driver steered too hard or braked too hard, the car would adapt. One of the positions BMW adopts is that the car understands not only the driver but the road, and the conditions.

Once the copilot role was decided, they asked where he came from. Since it was a German car, should it have a German voice? Nass said, "The fear there was that there were stereotypes associated with that particular accent, so that was ruled out." This was an interesting example of applied stereotyping—the assumption that affluent Americans are happy to buy German cars for their prestige, status, and fine engineering, but not if they talk with a German accent! But then, some Americans won't buy a German car because they will not forget the Holocaust. There may even be Americans who would like a car that talks with a sultry German voice, like, say, Marlene Dietrich's. To each his stereotype!

There was discussion of different American accents, and where in this country the BMW voice should come from, and some were rejected. The range of personalities considered is fascinating. Cliff generated about twenty-five models, from Night Rider to Hal the computer in the movie *2001*, to the buck on the stagecoach, "a sort of wacky older guy who rode shotgun, to a golfing buddy, and so on." Then they listened to hundreds of thousands of voices to come up with those that sounded like a copilot: male, slightly younger than the average age of the driver, so drivers wouldn't feel threatened. A masculine voice, but not overtly masculine. In the actual voice chosen, the frequency range and the pitch were a little higher than one would expect from a pilot, and in fact it's higher-pitched than the average demographic of the BMW user, so that the owner could still feel highly masculine and in control. All this information came from the company's research, Cliff said; "in fact, car companies have always been in the lead in truly understanding their customers."

The human brain is finely attuned to differences in language choice that marks status, ethnicity, region, and so on, Nass said, and "the same rules and expectations play out even in a car."

Most people are most comfortable with speech that matches their own. They particularly like speech and machines that will adapt to be more like them. "So, if it starts out speaking with a different cadence or rhythm or speech than you, then over time it matches yours, people love that." Machines can do exactly what one person does with another. "When you and I speak, our speech rhythms will begin to coincide in a process called alignment," he said. "So we start talking more like each other. We do it, of course, automatically. Computers can detect that."

In fact, the voice in the BMW sounded quite determined, even a little stentorian to our ears, and did not always understand our requests. It frequently said, "Pardon me?" Cliff said, "Our research shows that if the car says, 'I'm sorry, I didn't understand you,' people *believe* that modesty," and conclude that the technology doesn't work. In experiments with different "blame systems," the "self-blame" voice was really liked for being modest but thought to be dumb, while the user-blame system was smart but hated: "if it blames you and says, 'You must speak more clearly, you must, you know, shape up,' that's a rather aggressive response." The perfect solution turned out to be the no-blame system, in which a copilot would simply say, " 'There is a problem, I'm alerting you to it; you are the judge of how to solve the problem'—hence, *Pardon me.*"

Nass says: "Current and future voice interfaces are not likely to acquire the same capabilities as humans. So—systematic experimentation can point to clever 'tricks' to disguise the system's ignorance of, or inability to obey, social rules. In sum, to ensure that we could successfully design voice interfaces not just for cars but also for voice-based e-commerce, stock checking and purchase, technical support, virtual secretaries, appliances, and toys, we combined the psychology of human-human interaction with our own research on how people think and feel about voice-based interfaces."

As prices for these systems fall, there will be voice technology in all cars, he said, and waxed enthusiastic imagining a voice for a VW Beetle: "It would be a very present, rich voice, almost certainly female, because of the nature of the curviness of the car, and a great deal of enthusiasm and energy, and, you know, not too flighty, because, after all, it is a car." What would women think of that stereotyping—buy a Hummer?

Nass believes there will be a spread of voice technologies from higher- to lower-end things, and with this proliferation will come the issues of how we integrate them—"or do we want a cacophony of voices in our home screaming for attention?"

God, we thought, you get home after a hard day and fifteen things in the house are talking to you?

"Exactly, and you have to design around that problem," Nass said. "It's not clear that people are going to want to have long conversations with their toasters or refrigerators. But at the same time, it's very useful that technologies say, 'Hey, you know, my batteries are getting low, fix me.' "

We thanked Cliff and the obliging BMW rep who let us drive his machine for a while on the coastal highway, stopping from time to time to contemplate the Pacific Ocean.

* * *

It was observed long ago that all American history is a transition from an Atlantic to a Pacific phase. Although American attention has recently been riveted on the Middle East, the Pacific phase of our destiny looms larger and larger. Wallace Stegner writes, "In the past generation or two, even our wars have gone Asian, along with much of our trade, some of our religious searching, and a lot of our apprehension." China provides an ever-growing share of goods that America imports. Vast new container ships known as PNXs, too large to transit the Panama Canal, now ply the Pacific between China, Taiwan, and South Korea and Portland, Oregon; Seattle, Washington; and Vancouver, British Columbia. Not just goods but financial and service industries are reaching across the Pacific. India has become a major partner of American companies wanting to *outsource* service jobs, like call centers.

The size of the Asian populations forces experts peering into the future to ask how long our language can remain dominant in the world. By the middle of the twenty-first century, when Americans born today will just be middle-aged, many predict the weight of numbers and economic power will make Chinese the dominant language. David Graddol of the English Company, a publishing and consulting firm, says that in 1995 English was the world's second-most-common native tongue, after Chinese. "By 2050, Chinese will remain predominant, with Hindi-Urdu of India and Arabic climbing past English among people 15–24, and Spanish nearly equal to it." Employers in parts of Asia were already looking beyond English, Graddol said. "In the next decade, the new 'must learn' language is likely to be Mandarin." Barbara Wallraff, a widely published writer on language issues, questions the frequent assumption that, because American culture furthers innovation and openness to new ideas, that culture is inseparable from the English language:

> Even if the vanguards in all scientific and technological fields, everywhere in the world, used English in their work, once the fruits of their labor became known to ordinary people and be-

gan to matter to them, people would coin words in their local languages to describe these things. Theoretical physicists at international conferences may speak English among themselves, but most high school and college physics teachers use their native languages in class with their students.

Some economists predict that when China's rate of economic development produces more consumers than America does for new products—computers, for example—then American makers of such products will begin to shift design priorities to that market. Until now, American manufacturers have designed for American consumers and sold those products to the rest of the world with minor local adjustments. Barbara Wallraff points out that the Microsoft engineers who designed the Windows computer-operating system spoke English, and used English in what they created, but the words that users see on the screen are available in twenty-eight languages—and the spell-checker offers a choice of four varieties of English.

Now, in the age of globalization, a time could come when it will make sense for an IBM or a Microsoft not only to manufacture in China but to design for China. If that seems a little far-fetched, consider that the biggest new thrust in computer research—speech recognition—drew some of its inspiration from the needs of Chinese computer users.

That is our reason for traveling now to Seattle, to visit the man considered by his peers to be the "superstar" of voice-recognition technology, Xuedong Huang, known to his colleagues as "XD." Microsoft, which is making a major investment in this field, has put XD in charge of its .NET Speech Technologies Group, located at the Redmond headquarters, outside Seattle.

On one of Seattle's misty mornings, we drove out to XD's home in suburban Bellevue, in a landscape dominated by fog-shrouded spruce trees, then chatted as he drove us on the scenic route along Sammamish

Lake to the Microsoft campus. His Lexus was fitted with its own navigation system, which was programmed to take him a more direct way, and a woman's voice kept breaking in to remind us. Cliff Nass was right about our tendency to treat talking computers like people. It was hard not to imagine this woman getting testy as she repeatedly tried to redirect XD to the route he usually took to work—all in our heads, of course.

XD grew up in China and took his bachelor's and master's degrees there, and a doctorate in engineering at the University of Edinburgh. Before joining Microsoft, he was on the faculty at Carnegie Mellon, where he directed the effort to develop a speech-recognition system. He was drawn to it because of the difficulty Chinese encountered in using computers. In Mandarin a literate person knows six thousand characters, but with no Chinese alphabet, the language cannot easily be entered through the twenty-six-button alphabetic keyboards of Western computers. That involves typing in a phonetic version of each Chinese word and having it converted to the Chinese character, a very laborious process. However, the characters are, of course, sounds in spoken Chinese, so, if the computers could grasp spoken language, it would make computer access much easier. That insight created a major impetus for research in China but in the West as well. Microsoft and others calculated that this could be the next major expansion of computer use, making the contact with a computer as easy as talking to family or friends. XD said, "Speech is the most natural way for people to get information."

Microsoft began this research ten years ago and has been reducing errors by about 10 percent a year. "With that rate," XD says, "computers should be able to recognize the human voice as accurately as humans do, in ten to twenty years. When that happens, the impact will be profound, really amazing."

There is still a long way to go. A fundamental part of the effort involves assembling a mammoth database of American English usage, printed and spoken. It includes twenty years of newspapers and the recorded conversation of fifty thousand people. From that, using statistical methods, a model is created, which computers will search in trying to recognize any sample of speech.

To create the model, and to analyze new speech, language is reduced to the smallest components of sound, starting with the basic distinctive elements, known as *phonemes,* then much smaller elements for which XD has coined the word *senone.* A *senone* represents a fragment of speech lasting ten milliseconds, or one-hundredth of a second, shown on the computer screen in wave form. Each of these is given a mathematical formula to create a Markov model, a method of calculating probability. Looking at the two previous words, the system then decides which word sequence would best match the spoken sounds it has been given and the linguistic model constructed from the database.

It is already working at a level satisfactory for some simple applications—for example, in telephone-company directory-assistance systems. They ask the caller to utter a small range of words in answer to simple questions like *What city? What listing?* So does the United Airlines flight-information service, which is reported to have saved the airline $25 million a year by replacing the people who used to answer the phones with a computer speech-recognition system. It places limited demands on the recognition technology. Callers are directed to say specific things like city names, dates, or flight numbers. But it has an accuracy rate of about 95 percent.

Amtrak's reservation service begins with a perky young female voice saying, "Hi, this is Amtrak. I'm Julie!" But, however casual and conversational she sounds, Julie the computer can understand only key words solicited by her prompts, such as "Okay, to get schedules and price information, say *schedule.*"

Microsoft and other software packages now allow people to dictate vocally to their computers, which convert the speech to text on the screen. They have the capacity to learn the user's own acoustic pattern, the rate of speech, and the intonation, and to adapt to that voice. XD Huang says that, using his company's products, he can dictate, for example, e-mail messages, and finish everything, including correcting the mistakes, almost twice as fast as he can using the keyboard.

These are relatively easy applications. It is far more difficult to have computers understand natural and casual human speech. There are several obstacles.

One is that English is a much harder language for computers to understand than Japanese, or Italian, or Spanish. There is an absurd inconsistency in how words sound and are spelled, which permits *through, threw, true,* and *too* all to rhyme, as do *cough* and *off, rough* and *ruff.* Some verbs may be nouns, and vice versa, identifiable only by their position in a sentence, as in *My drawing shows him drawing his bow.* There is also the complexity of our idioms. Any database would have to be rich in common idioms to avoid the charming mistakes one finds in public signs in non-English-speaking countries, such as this in a Norwegian cocktail lounge: "Ladies are requested not to have children in the bar." Or this in a hotel in Egypt: "Patrons need have no anxiety about the water. It has all been passed by the management."

For sophisticated usage, the database would have to have a vocabulary wider and more current than Microsoft's popular word-processing program, MS Word, whose spell-checker has limitations. It does not recognize, for example, the word *prescriptivist,* which is used frequently in this book, and which has appeared in the unabridged *Random House Dictionary* at least since 1983. Nor does it recognize proper names. The challenges are formidable. According to XD Huang, the greatest difficulty is getting a computer not just to recognize language but to have the intelligence to help you get your work done.

Another problem is understanding speech in a noisy environment, at which humans show amazing ability. This is a problem that makers of hearing aids also have yet to solve well, to enable their users to speak to one person at a party and not have the device confused by the sounds of other voices. Speech recognition achieves much lower error rates when it works in quiet settings, as in a phone call from a quiet office, but the error rate may be much higher when one is using a mobile phone in an airport concourse. Computers are better at recognizing formal or broadcast speech, or a text being read, and not nearly so good with informal, casual conversation. One mechanical solution is to improve the quality and number of microphones picking up the speech.

That still leaves what XD Huang and a colleague called in a recent paper "a very large performance gap between human and machine speech recognition" and an understanding among researchers of "the fragile nature of the current speech recognition system design." To counter that, a search is under way for novel approaches, finding an "architecture" different from the system we have described above.

It is obviously much harder to get machines to match the amazing human understanding of speech than it is to simulate or synthesize speech, as we saw in Cliff Nass's lab at Stanford.

If they are successful, XD Huang believes the impact will be "even more profound than television. Television is a passive way for people to communicate—they listen, they cannot participate."

The applications he calls "amazing" will change the way people work and communicate. But the examples he gave—calling from a car to have a florist deliver flowers to one's wife, or calling ahead to a pharmacy to request a prescription—seem relatively simple tasks, performable with cell phones today. The enormous investment being made to master this challenging technology suggests that Microsoft expects a much bigger payback—millions of new customers for computers and software.

Linguistically, it also raises the question of for whom, for what parts of the population, this investment is being made. As we have seen, Americans speak with many different accents, and that variety does not seem to be disappearing. Some of those accents are difficult for other Americans to understand. The police chief in Shreveport, Louisiana, complained that their voice-recognition system to route nonemergency calls did not understand the local accent! XD said his technology is tuned to everyone's voice. "Microsoft is committed to providing technology that will meet the needs of everyone, no matter what their background is, no matter what accent they have."

But right now, like so many Americans, he believes that people from the Midwest would have the best chance of being understood: "It is true that today's technology has its limitations. It works better for people who speak standard American English." XD believes that TV played a "huge role in homogenizing the accent, and people have been listening to the TV voice, the standard American English, all along. But people are not participating. They are not responding to the voice. With speech interaction, we can actually have people participate, so this will be two-way communication. This is why the impact will be more profound. We will see a nice convergence between technology and society." We pointed out what all the linguists have told us, that a lot of people listening to television may have a passive understanding of standard English but continue to speak with a strong local accent. Will the computers understand their accents, or would people have to speak standard English?

People can adapt, XD said, and gave himself as an example. "I have an accent and I have been interacting with computers without any problem. When people interact with computers, they will carefully select the word, use the right tone and the rate of speech, because they want to focus on getting the task done, so it will be important for them to improve their accent, in a sense. So—we'll see the convergence, machine and the society and the culture. I believe the diversity will maintain. But the people will eventually probably converge to the voice, helping them to interact with the machines better. Just like me. This by no means indicates that I have eliminated my accent."

At one point in our conversations, XD suggested that if people sounded like CNN, computers would understand them easily. But he amended that to say, "If you use standard American English, probably you will get the work done easier, faster."

We came away from Microsoft with the conviction that if speech recognition reaches the level of sophistication XD promises, it will apply interesting new pressure on Americans to standardize their English—at least while in conversation with their computers.

Barbara Wallraff says this may well matter to the future of English: "The more we need to use English to communicate with machines—or with people whose fluency is limited, or whose understanding of English does not coincide with ours—the more simplified the language will need to be."

How simplified and how standard this coming computer "revolution" will require our language to be are open questions. So is the matter we discussed with Cliff Nass, the stereotypes that are deeply lodged in the linguistic psyche of America. Will corporations looking to employ speech recognition as soon as possible to replace real human beings find it profitable to insist on technology so sophisticated that it will understand all American accents, or will it pay them to go to XD Huang's convergence model—make people adapt to the computer, not the computer to people? As we have seen in this journey, in many people's minds the idea is ingrained that some American dialects and accents are "unnecessary," that if people would just "speak properly" there wouldn't be a problem—which usually means if they would just speak like educated Midwesterners. If commerce increasingly forces people to talk to computers, will they be as disenfranchised, left out of the new economy, as many are now when they speak the "unnecessary" dialects of America? Ultimately the answers to these questions will be marketing decisions, but decisions that could have social side effects, or, in Pentagonese, *collateral damage.*

Everything in the American experience—each new frontier encountered, geographical, spiritual, technological—has altered our language. What kind of a frontier are we crossing by teaching computers our most fundamental human skill, to speak?

Will we all end up talking like computers? Hardly. History, human nature, and what we have learned in this journey through American English suggest otherwise. In the future there will be competing linguistic trends, John Baugh said as he discussed the choices that shaped his own life: "For ordinary people, not professionals, there will be a tendency to maintain their regional or ethnic identities. And so those who live in Louisiana and Texas who feel strongly that their vernacular is a reflection of their loyalty to their culture, they're going to maintain that. But for individuals who feel that the way they speak somehow stigmatizes them and restricts their opportunities, they're clearly going to want to change."

* * *

What is the future of American English? If the trends we have identified stay on their present paths, we can expect to see more diversity in regional speech patterns, new dialects becoming stronger (as in California), some disappearing (as in Ocracoke), and some continuing to diverge from standard American (as African American English). Yet we can also expect to see convergence, in the sense that, while the media do not homogenize dialects, they do condition speakers of all dialects to hear and understand others. That may even produce more tolerance and appreciation of the linguistic diversity of this country, and less negative stereotyping of some dialects (such as New York or Southern) as "bad English." Thus we can expect our language to obey two seemingly contradictory influences, both centrifugal and centripetal, its universe both expanding and contracting.

Also, given the increasing racial and ethnic diversity of the country, and ongoing immigration, we can expect our version of English to be continually modified by and to borrow from all the immigrant languages, as it has done throughout American history.

Our language reflects our society; "not a system separate from the people who speak it," it is the expression of the people who use it: "The people are prior to the language," says linguist Connie Eble. Many Americans have cast off certain formalities of dress and comportment, as has the language. We are obsessed with youth and defer to its tastes, and the language shows that. We are endlessly creative, and that innovation in all fields constantly generates fresh language, considered slang or jargon when new, but soon made respectable or it disappears. We countenance a franker view of sex than recent generations and are more explicit in discussing it. Expletives once not heard in public appear in movies and on radio and television. Calling 2003 the "Four-Letter Summer," the *New York Observer* said: "Once the English language's most shocking, egregious, off limits word, it has become just another cultural noise, thrown around with the casualness of a summer softball, appearing on your TV, on your answering machine, at a newsstand near you, from the mouth of your son, your mom, your Congressman, your philosophy professor, your dentist, your waiter, your innocent virgin on the street." But there are backlashes. When Bono, lead singer of the band U2, received a Golden Globe Award, his comment that winning was "fuckin' brilliant" was broadcast live. After protests, the Federal Communications Commission excused it, saying Bono used it as an adverb, not to describe a sexual act. Later, however, the commission overturned that decision, and launched a drive— backed by Congress with heavy fines—to cleanse the airwaves of vulgarity. Bono told the *New York Times*, "I guess I don't speak American, but I thought I did. . . . If you're Irish, you love language, and if you do, you're going to fall on the occasional expletive; it's the percussive side of the language." If so, American language is becoming a lot more percussive. In June 2004—on the Senate floor—Vice President Dick Cheney told Democratic senator Patrick Leahy to "fuck off" or "go fuck yourself," according to congressional aides.

While some public language grows saltier, American society has become more respectful of women, minorities, Native Americans, the elderly, the handicapped, and somewhat more tolerant of gays—and the language reflects all that.

America is still racist to a degree; so are attitudes toward language, especially African American English. Linguist Dennis Baron says that "linguistic discrimination remains publicly acceptable in the United States, while other forms of discrimination do not."

The corollary to all these trends is a fashion for political correctness, a certain bending-over-backward not to offend. That is apparent in the language, as is the satirical send-up of it.

Despite the amazing uniformity of our national tastes in clothing, fast-food chains, movies, and television, we preserve our regional flavor, and so does language.

Our restless population continues to mix things up—"hooked on change," in Wallace Stegner's phrase. We are constantly moving, Midwesterners to the Southwest, African Americans back south, one-seventh of the population (forty-two million people) changing homes each year. Immigration continues; so does racial and ethnic mixing. As fashion finds new chic in multiracial features, we are increasingly saying, like the girl we overheard in the New York elevator, "You're cute. What's your mix?"

Most of this probably would not surprise and much of it might delight Walt Whitman, whom we quoted at the beginning, appealing for a language of "unhemmed latitude." We feel we cannot sum up better

than with Whitman, who more than a century ago, in his famous trib-
ute to "Slang in America," delivered this judgment:

> Language, be it remember'd, is not an abstract construction of
> the learn'd, or of dictionary-makers, but is something arising
> out of the work, needs, ties, joys, affections, tastes, of long gen-
> erations of humanity, and has its bases broad and low, close to
> the ground. Its final decisions are made by the masses, people
> nearest the concrete, having most to do with actual land and
> sea.

Today, that seems as true as ever, and, like, how cool is that!

ACKNOWLEDGMENTS
★

In addition to the many linguists listed on pages 211–12, who gave their time and knowledge so generously to the television series and this book, the authors wish to thank others who contributed significantly.

The television series was a coproduction of MacNeil-Lehrer Productions and Paladin-InVision Productions, with Robert MacNeil the on-camera reporter and William Cran the director-producer. Intellectually we traveled together, and the series and this book are collaborations. We acknowledge the many contributions of Susan Mills, executive producer for MacNeil-Lehrer Productions, in Arlington, Virginia, whose persistence secured vital funding for the TV series, and we are grateful for the support and backing of Clive Syddall, executive producer for Paladin-InVision Productions, of London, England. Annette Miller and her research staff at MLP gave us invaluable help.

Our work benefits from the early research of Vivian Ducat, a colleague from *The Story of English,* who helped identify many of the themes and the linguists we feature. We are grateful to Christopher Buchanan, our associate producer, whose on-the-ground research, location scouting, and early interviewing were indispensable, and to Greg Barker, who directed one leg of our journey across America. We thank Tammy Robinson, vice president, and Jody Sheff, executive producer at

WNET/Channel 13 in New York, for their assistance, as well as Mary Beth Rogers and Dick Peterson of KLRU TV in Austin, Texas, for their early interest and support.

Finally, this book owes much to the insights and editing skills of our publisher, Nan A. Talese, and to the diligence of our copy editor, Terry Zaroff-Evans, at Doubleday.

NOTES

★

Works cited will be found in the Bibliography.

INTRODUCTION
Page
1. Adams is quoted in John Algeo, "America Is Ruining the English Language," in Bauer and Trudgill, eds.
2. Shaw's remark is quoted in *Reader's Digest*, Nov. 1942, p. 100.
2. Mencken, p. 224.
3. The estimate of one-fifth is attributed to linguist Steven Pinker by Nunberg, p. 151.
4. MacArthur, *Oxford Guide*, p. 165.
4. Warren Hoge, "Latest Word: 'Klingons' In, 'Muggles' Not Quite," *New York Times International*, Nov. 12, 2002.
5. Aldous Huxley, "Words and Their Meaning," in Black, ed., p. 1.

CHAPTER ONE—*The Language Wars*
Page
9. Fowler, p. 625.
10. Dennis Baron interview. Unless published works are cited, all quotations are from interviews by the authors for the PBS series *Do You Speak American?* © MacNeil-Lehrer Productions 2005.
10. Bill Manson, "Wordplay: Charles Harrington Elster at Home," *San Diego Home/Garden Lifestyles* magazine, Nov. 2002.
11. Simon, p. xiv.
13. Wilson, pp. 12–13.
13. Safire, *What's the Good Word*, p. 226.
13. Simon, p. 24.

14. Jespersen, p. 251.
14. Twain cited by Mencken, p. 72.
14. Whitman cited by Mencken, p. 74.
15. The most comprehensive and current work on slang is the *Random House Historical Dictionary of American Slang*, J. E. Lighter, ed.
16. Many of Nunberg's commentaries appear in *The Way We Talk Now*, this observation on p. 9.
16. Geoffrey Nunberg, "The Decline of Grammar," *Atlantic Monthly*, vol. 252, no. 6 (Dec. 1983).
16. Mark Halpern, "The War That Never Ends," *Atlantic*, vol. 279, no. 3 (March 1997).
17. Shachtman, p. 259.
17. McWhorter, p. 82.
21. The two examples are from *New York Times*, Jan. 2, 2004, p. A12; Nov. 20, 2002, p. A18.
24. John Rosenthal, "Corpus Linguistics," On Language, *New York Times Magazine*, Aug. 8, 2002.
27. Nunberg, p. 45.
28. King, Smith, and Phillips were quoted in "Vanishing Verbs," a report by Terence Smith on *The NewsHour with Jim Lehrer*, PBS, Aug. 24, 2001.
28. Geoffrey Nunberg, "Cablespeak: I Seeing the News Today, Oh Boy!" *New York Times*, "Review of the Week," Sunday, Dec. 8, 2002.

CHAPTER TWO—*Changing Dialects: Dingbatters Versus Hoi-Toiders*
Page
33. The Ocracoke story is told by Walt Wolfram, "Dialect in Danger," *American Language Review*, Nov.–Dec. 2000.
34. The Smith Island story is told by Natalie Schilling-Estes, "Fighting the Tide," *Language* magazine, June 2002.
35. Wolfram told the story in conversation with the authors.
37. Wolfram interview with authors.
38. Labov, *Principles*, vol. 2, p. 285.
38. Matthew V. Gordon, "Straight Talking from the Heartland," *Language* magazine, Jan. 2002.
40. These anecdotes were supplied by Labov in e-mails to the authors.
40. Labov's theory about women appears in detail in his *Principles*, vol. 2, pp. 279–84.
41. The Celeste story appears in Labov, pp. 386–95.
43. J. K. Chambers, "TV Makes People Sound the Same," in Bauer and Trudgill, eds., p. 124.
44. These words from McCool, *Pittsburghese*.

CHAPTER THREE—*Toward a Standard: Putting the "R" in "American"*
Page

51. The department-store research appears in Labov, *Principles of Linguistic Change*, vol. 1, chap. 4, "The Study of Change in Progress: Observations in Real Time."

52. Jones, *Accent on Privilege*, p. 123.

56. Bonfiglio, pp. 181–227.

59. Labov, *Principles*, vol. 2, p. 4.

63. Nunberg, p. 191.

63. Dowis and Wallace, pp. 2–6.

66. Vidal, Foreword.

CHAPTER FOUR—*This Ain't Your Mama's South Anymore*
Page

70. "I'm Inspired," music and lyrics by Cody James, © Cody James 2003.

71. This account is taken from John Fought, "Coastal and Inland Southern Speech: Rless and Rful," essay for the Web site http://macneil-lehrer.com/Speak/internal_docs for the TV series *Do You Speak American?*

72. Crawford Feagin's observations are from our interview. For her original study, see Bibliography.

76. Douglas Brinkley, "A Place in the Sun," in "Southern Exposure," *Financial Times* special report, Sept. 24, 2003.

77. Lenny Bruce is quoted ibid.

81. Jan Tillery and Guy Bailey, "Texas English," *Language*, Nov. 2003, pp. 43–45.

82. Those requiring further instruction can consult Kinky Friedman, *Guide to Texas Etiquette.*

84. Johnstone and Bean, pp. 7–11.

CHAPTER FIVE—*Hispanic Immigration: Reconquest or Assimilation?*
Page

90. Translation of Elena Poniatowska published by *Free Republic* ("A Conservative News Forum"), Aug. 11, 2001; original published in *El Imparcial*, Caracas, Venezuela, July 4, 2001: *"El pueblo de los pobres, los piojosos y las cucarachas está avanzando en Estados Unidos, un país que quiere hablar español porque hay 33,5 milliones de hispanos que imponen su cultura. México va recuperando los territorios cedidos a Estados Unidos con tácticas migratorias."*

91. Richard Rodriguez, "Dawn's Early Light," essay, *NewsHour with Jim Lehrer*, PBS, Jan. 30, 2004.

93. These examples come from Robert McCrum, William Cran, and Robert MacNeil; and Bill Bryson, *Made in America.*

94. The Franklin quotation and the fate of the German language in America come from Dennis Baron, chap. 3, "Defending the Native Tongue."

95. For the "Good English" campaign, see Baron, p. 155.

97. Bailon quoted in *American Journalism Review*, Oct. 2003.

103. Maryland and Virginia immigration in *Washington Post*, June 19, 2003.

103. Baron, preface, p. xiii.

104. Hanson quoted in Roger Clegg, "Here but Only Halfway," BookShelf, *Wall Street Journal*, June 19, 2003.

104. Samuel P. Huntington, "The Hispanic Challenge," *Foreign Policy*, March–April 2004.

105. David Brooks, "The Americano Dream" *New York Times*, Op-Ed Page, Feb. 24, 2004.

105. Alistair Cooke, "Foreword," and S. I. Hayakawa, "Introduction," to Fernando de la Peña, *Democracy or Babel*.

106. Baron, p. 189.

110. For a fuller account, see Carmen Fought's essay "How Social Situations Affect Language Structure," on the Web site http://macneil-lehrer.com/Speak/ internal_docs for the TV series *Do You Speak American?*

CHAPTER SIX—*Bad-mouthing Black English*

Page

116. Smitherman, p. 52.

116. Descriptions of Black English quoted by Nunberg, p. 118.

116. Mencken, p. 71.

117. There is a full account of the *creole theory* in Dillard, *Black English*.

118. Conroy, p. 3.

120. Bailey and Cukor-Avila, chap. 2.

123. Laura's talk was transcribed in Bailey, Cukor-Avila, and Maynor, eds., p. 61.

125. Rupert and Slim quoted in Cukor-Avila and Bailey, "An Approach to Sociolinguistic Fieldwork," pp. 169–70.

127. These examples are from Baugh's unpublished fieldwork.

127. Labov, *Principles*, vol. 2, p. 7.

128. Raspberry, quoted in Nunberg, p. 119.

128. Baugh, *Beyond Ebonics*, p. 58.

128. Labov Senate testimony quoted by Baugh, p. 59.

128. Cukor-Avila, "Complex Grammatical History," p. 83.

129. McWhorter, *Doing Our Own Thing*, p. 213.

129. James Baldwin, "If Black English Isn't a Language, Then Tell Me, What Is?" *New York Times*, July 29, 1979.

131. Baugh, *Beyond Ebonics*, p. 5.

131. Ibid., pp. 5–6.

133. William Raspberry, "Black English," *Washington Post*, July 13, 1979.

133. Carl T. Rowan, "Black English Ruling Lambasted," *Detroit News*, Aug. 5, 1979.

133. Baldwin, *New York Times,* July 29, 1979.

134. Baugh, *Beyond Ebonics,* p. 28.

134. Ibid., p. 50.

134. "gibberish . . ." and Nunberg's response in Nunberg, p. 118.

136. "Barely Audible," in Chinaka Hodge.

138. Details of this program are in LeMoine, *English for Your Success.*

140. Baugh, *Beyond Ebonics,* p. 104.

140. Renée Blake and Cecilia Cutler, "AAVE and Variation in Teachers' Attitudes: A Question of Social Philosophy?," paper prepared for Linguistics Department, New York University, 2000.

141. Felicia R. Lees, *New York Times,* Jan. 7, 1994.

144. H. Samy Alim, "Street Conscious Copula Variation in the Hip Hop Nation," paper written for the Web site http://macneil-lehrer.com/Speak/internal_docs for the TV series *Do You Speak American?*

144. Whoopi Goldberg quoted in Baz Dreisinger, "The Whitest Black Girl on TV," *New York Times,* Sept. 28, 2003.

147. William Safire, "Bling, Bling," On Language, *New York Times Magazine,* Nov. 23, 2003, p. 28.

147. Dreisinger, *New York Times,* Sept. 28, 2003.

148. McWhorter, p. 232.

148. On the migration of blacks back to the South, see Frey.

CHAPTER SEVEN—*Language from a State of Change*
Page

152. This provenance for the name California comes from the *Encyclopaedia Britannica,* 2004.

152. Diane Johnson, "False Promises," a review of Joan Didion's *Where I Was From, New York Times Book Review,* Dec. 4, 2003.

153. Jack Kerouac, "Essentials of Spontaneous Prose," reproduced on Blues for Peace Web site.

154. Penelope Eckert and Norma Mendoza-Denton, "Getting Real in the Golden State," *Language,* March 2002, pp. 29–30.

155. Song and lyrics by Frank Zappa, performed by Moon Unit, from the album *Ship Arriving Too Late to Save a Drowning Witch,* released May 1982.

156. Eckert quoted in Lisa M. Krieger, "Teen Girls Defining a California Dialect," *Mercury News,* San Jose, Calif., Feb. 8, 2004.

161. Cited by Eckert and Mendoza-Denton, p. 30.

161. Readers who wish to add to the survey may do so through its Web site— http://hcs.harvard.edu/~golder/dialect/staticmaps/state—adding in the abbreviation for their own state.

166. See Werner and Badillo, *Skateboarder's Start-Up* and *Skateboarding: New Levels.*

167. *Skateboarder's Start-Up*, p. 67.

168. "The Ten Most Beautiful Women at Princeton," *New Yorker*, May 27, 2002.

169. Stephen Levy, "He's Like 'Do it now!' and I'm Like 'No!'" *English Today*, Jan. 2003, pp. 24–32.

CHAPTER EIGHT—*Teaching Computers to Speak American*
Page

181. For more on these experiments, see Cliff Nass, "Machine Voices: Creating a Synthetic Language for BMW," paper on Web site, http://macneil-lehrer.com/Speak/internal_docs, for the TV series *Do You Speak American?*

182. Reeves and Nass, p. 12.

190. Stegner, p. 140.

190. Graddol quoted by Randolph E. Schmid, "English Won't Reign, Researcher Predicts," *Philadelphia Inquirer*, March 5, 2004.

190. Barbara Wallraff, "What Global Language?" *Atlantic*, Nov. 2000, p. 66.

195. Li Deng and Xuedong Huang, "Challenges in Adopting Speech Recognition," *Communications of the ACM,* Jan. 2004, pp. 69–75.

197. Wallraff, p. 66.

199. Alexandra Jacobs and Maria Russo, "It's a Four-Letter Summer: The F-Word as New 'Gosh!' Commerce, Fashion Make *Verboten* Curse Conversational Paprika," *New York Observer,* July 7–14, 2003.

199. Bono quoted by Frank Rich, "Après Janet, a Deluge," *New York Times*, Sunday, March 21, 2004.

200. Baron, p. 191.

200. Stegner, p. 204.

201. Whitman, "Slang in America," from *Whitman: Complete Poetry and Collected Prose* (New York: Library of America, 1982), p. 1166.

LINGUISTS CONSULTED
★

Following are the names and affiliations of the linguists consulted for this book and in the making of the PBS TV series *Do You Speak American?* The names in **bold type** are those of a core group who advised us; the others are scholars we consulted.

Guy Bailey, Ph.D. Provost, University of Texas at San Antonio.

Richard Bailey, Ph.D. Professor of English Language and Literature, University of Michigan, Ann Arbor.

Dennis Baron, Ph.D. Head, Department of English, Professor of English and Linguistics, University of Illinois at Urbana-Champaign.

John Baugh, Ph.D. Professor of Education and Linguistics, School of Education, Stanford University, Palo Alto, California.

Charles Boberg, Ph.D. Department of Linguistics, McGill University, Montreal, Quebec, Canada.

Mary Bucholtz, Ph.D. Department of Linguistics, University of California at Santa Barbara.

Ronald R. Butters, Ph.D. English Department, Duke University, Durham, N.C.

J. K. Chambers, Ph.D. Department of Linguistics, University of Toronto, Canada.

Patricia Cukor-Avila, English Department, University of North Texas, Denton.

Cecilia Cutler, Ph.D. candidate. New York University.

Bethany Kay Dumas, J.D. and Ph.D. Professor of English and Chair, IDP Linguistics Committee, University of Tennessee, Knoxville.

Connie C. Eble, Ph.D. Professor of English, English Department, University of North Carolina, Chapel Hill.

Penelope Eckert, Ph.D. English Department, Stanford University, Palo Alto, Calif.

Crawford Feagin, Ph.D. Research Associate, Linguistics Laboratory, University of Pennsylvania, Philadelphia.

Michael Forman, Ph.D. Chair, Department of Linguistics, and Associate Professor and Acting Chair of the Graduate Faculty, University of Hawaii at Manoa, Honolulu.

Carmen Fought, Ph.D. Assistant Professor of Linguistics, Pitzer College, Diamond Bar, Calif.

John Fought, Ph.D. Director of Business Development, Language Systems, Inc., Pomona College, Claremont, Calif.

Mary Ellen Garcia, Ph.D. Department of Modern Languages and Literatures, University of Texas at San Antonio.

John Holm, Ph.D. Hunter College, City University of New York.

Edward Ives, Ph.D. Professor Emeritus of Folklore, University of Maine, Orono.

Barbara Johnstone, Ph.D. Professor of Rhetoric, Department of English, Carnegie Mellon University, Pittsburgh, Pa.

Braj Kachru, Ph.D. Department of Linguistics, University of Illinois at Urbana-Champaign.

Robert D. King, Ph.D. Rapoport Chair of Jewish Studies, University of Texas at Austin.

William Labov, Ph.D. Professor of Linguistics and Director of the *Atlas of North American English*, University of Pennsylvania, Philadelphia.

Donald Lance, Ph.D. Professor Emeritus of English, University of Missouri–Columbia.

William Leap, Ph.D. Department of Anthropology, American University, Washington, D.C.

David Lightfoot, Ph.D. Dean, Graduate School of Arts and Sciences, Georgetown University, Washington, D.C.

Peter Lowenberg, Ph.D. Associate Professor, San Jose State University, Campbell, Calif.

Allan Metcalf, Ph.D. Executive Secretary, American Dialect Society; English Department, MacMurray College, Jacksonville, Ill.

Patricia Nichols, Ph.D. Professor Emeritus, Linguistics and Language Development, San Jose State University, Campbell, Calif.

Dennis R. Preston, Ph.D. Professor of Linguistics, Michigan State University, East Lansing.

John Rickford, Ph.D. Department of Linguistics, Stanford University, Palo Alto, Calif.

Maurice Scharton, Ph.D. Professor of English, Illinois State University (deceased).

Natalie Schilling-Estes, Ph.D. Assistant Professor of Linguistics, Georgetown University, Washington, D.C.

Edgar Schneider, Ph.D. Institut für Anglistik, Universität Regensburg, Germany.

Jesse Sheidlower, Editor-at-Large, North American Editorial Unit, *Oxford English Dictionary*.

Lawrence Smith, Ph.D. Christopher, Smith & Associates, LLC, Kane'ohe, Hawaii.

Geneva Smitherman, Ph.D. Distinguished Professor of English, Michigan State University, East Lansing.

Deborah Tannen, Ph.D. Department of Linguistics, Georgetown University, Washington, D.C.

Kenneth Wilson, Ph.D. University of Connecticut, Storrs (deceased).

Walt Wolfram, Ph.D. Professor of English, English Department, North Carolina State University, Raleigh.

BIBLIOGRAPHY

✪

Bailey, Guy, and Patricia Cukor-Avila. "The Sociohistorical Context." Chap. 2 in *The Development of African American English Since 1850: The Evolution of a Grammar.* Cambridge: University Press, 2005 (in press).

Bailey, Guy, Patricia Cukor-Avila, and Natalie Maynor, eds. *The Emergence of Black English.* Philadelphia: John Benjamins Publishing Company, 1991.

Baron, Dennis. *The English-Only Question: An Official Language for Americans?* New Haven: Yale University Press, 1990.

Bauer, Laurie, and Peter Trudgill, eds. *Language Myths.* New York: Penguin Books, 1998.

Baugh, John. *Beyond Ebonics: Linguistic Pride and Racial Prejudice.* New York: Oxford University Press, 2000.

————. *Out of the Mouths of Slaves.* Austin: University of Texas Press, 1999.

Bender, James F. *The NBC Handbook of Pronunciation.* New York: Thomas Y. Crowell, 1943.

Black, Max, ed. *The Importance of Language.* Englewood Cliffs, N.J.: Prentice Hall, 1962.

Bonfiglio, Thomas Paul. *Race and the Rise of Standard American.* New York: Mouton de Gruyter, 2002.

Bryson, Bill. *Made in America: An Informal History of the English Language in the United States.* New York: Perennial, 2001.

————. *The Mother Tongue: English and How It Got That Way.* New York: Perennial, 2001.

Cassidy, Frederick G., and Joan Houston Hall, eds. *Dictionary of American Regional English.* Vol. I. Cambridge, Mass.: Belknap Press of Harvard University Press, 1985. Subsequent volumes in 1991, 1996, and 2002. Volume V is in press.

Ciardi, John. *Good Words to You: An All-New Dictionary and Native's Guide to the Unknown American Language.* New York: Harper & Row, 1987.

Conroy, Pat. *The Water Is Wide.* New York: Bantam, 1994.

Cooke, Alistair, "Foreword," and S. I. Hayakawa, "Introduction." In Fernando de la Peña, *Democracy or Babel: The Case for Official English.* Washington, D.C.: U.S. English, 1991.

Cukor-Avila, Patricia. "Co-Existing Grammars: The Relationship Between the Evolution of African American and White Vernacular English in the South." Chap. 4 in *Sociocultural and Historical Contexts of African American English*. Philadelphia: John Benjamins, 2001.

————. "The Complex Grammatical History of African American and White Vernaculars in the South." Chap. 5 in Stephen J. Nagle and Sara L. Sanders, *English in the Southern United States*. Cambridge: Cambridge University Press, 2003.

Cukor-Avila, Patricia, and Guy Bailey. "An Approach to Sociolingistic Fieldwork: A Site Study of Rural AAVE in a Texas Community." In *English Worldwide* (Amsterdam: John Benjamins, 1995).

Dillard, J. L. *American Talk*. New York: Random House, 1976.

————. *Black English: Its History and Usage in the United States*. New York: Random House, 1972.

Dowis, Richard, and James J. Wallace. *SPELL Member Handbook*. Fourth ed., 2003. SPELL, P.O. Box 321, Braselton, Ga. 30517.

Eckert, Penelope. *Jocks and Burnouts: Social Categories and Identity in the High School*. New York: Teachers College Press, 1989.

Feagin, Crawford. *Variation and Change in Alabama English: A Sociolinguistic Study of the White Community*. Washington, D.C.: Georgetown University Press, 1979.

Ferguson, Charles A., and Shirley Brice Heath, eds. *Language in the USA*. Cambridge: Cambridge University Press, 1981.

Follett, Wilson. *Modern American Usage: A Guide*. Rev. by Erik Wensberg. New York: Hill & Wang, 1998.

Fowler, H. W. *Modern English Usage*. 1926. Second ed. rev. and ed. by Sir Ernest Gowers. Oxford: Oxford University Press, 1965.

Frey, William H. *Census 2000 Shows Large Black Return to the South, Reinforcing the Region's "White-Black" Demographic Profile*. Population Studies Center Research Report No. 01-473. Institute for Social Research, University of Michigan, May 2001.

Friedman, Kinky. *Guide to Texas Etiquette: How to Get to Heaven or Hell, Without Going Through Dallas–Fort Worth*. New York: HarperCollins, 2001.

Garner, Bryan A. *The Oxford Dictionary of American Usage and Syle*. New York: Oxford University Press, 2000.

Hodge, Chinaka. *Know These Limbs: Writings by Chinaka Hodge*. poetess02@yahoo.com is her Web address.

Ivins, Molly. *Molly Ivins Can't Say That, Can She?* New York: Random House, 1991.

Jespersen, Otto. *The Growth and Structure of the English Language*. 1905. Ninth ed. New York: Doubleday Anchor, 1955.

Johnstone, Barbara, and Dan Baumgardt. "Yinzburg Online: Vernacular Norming in a Conversation About Dialect, Place, and Identity." Unpublished paper produced for Rhetoric Program, Department of English, Carnegie Mellon University, Pittsburgh, Pa. 15213-3890.

Johnstone, Barbara, and Judith Mattson Bean. "Self-Expression and Linguistic Variation." *Language in Society*, 26 (1997): 221–46.

Jones, Katharine W. *Accent on Privilege*. Philadelphia: Temple University Press, 2001.

Labov, William. "The Logic of Nonstandard English." *Georgetown Monograph Series on Languages and Linguistics*. Washington, D.C.: Georgetown University Press, 1969.

————. *Principles of Linguistic Change*. Vol. 1, *Internal Factors*. Oxford: Blackwell, 1994.

————. *Principles of Linguistic Change*. Vol. 2, *Social Factors*. Oxford: Blackwell, 2001.

Labov, William, Sharon Ash, and Charles Boberg. *Atlas of North American English*. New York: Mouton de Gruyter, 2005 (in press).

LeMoine, Noma. *English for Your Success: A Language Development Program for African American Children, Curriculum Guide for Grades 4–5*. Maywood, N.J.: Peoples Publishing Group, 1999.

Lighter, J. E., ed. *Random House Historical Dictionary of American Slang*. Vols. I and II. Jesse Sheidlower, project editor. Vol. I, New York: Random House, 1994–97. Vol. III forthcoming.

MacArthur, Tom. *Oxford Guide to World English*. New York: Oxford University Press, 2002.

Marckwardt, Albert H. *American English*. Second ed., rev. by J. L. Dillard. New York: Oxford University Press, 1980.

McCool, Sam. *Sam McCool's New Pittsburghese*. Pittsburgh: Goodwill Industries of Pittsburgh, 1982.

McCrum, Robert, William Cran, and Robert MacNeil. *The Story of English*. New York: Penguin Books, 2003.

McWhorter, John. *Doing Our Own Thing: The Degradation of Language and Music and Why We Should, Like, Care*. New York: Gotham Books, 2003.

Mencken, H. L. *The American Language*. New York: Alfred A. Knopf, 2000.

Metcalf, Allan. *Predicting New Words: The Secrets of Their Success*. New York: Houghton Mifflin, 2002.

Newman, Edwin. *Strictly Speaking: Will America Be the Death of English?* Indianapolis: Bobbs-Merrill, 1974.

Niedzielski, Nancy, and Dennis R. Preston. *Folk Linguistics*. New York: Mouton de Gruyter, 2003.

Nunberg, Geoffrey. *The Way We Talk Now*. Boston: Houghton Mifflin, 2001.

Popcorn, Faith, and Adam Hanft. *Dictionary of the Future*. New York: Hyperion, 2001.

Reeves, Byron, and Clifford Nass. *The Media Equation: How People Treat Computers, Television, and New Media like Real People and Places*. New York: Cambridge University Press, 1998.

Safire, William. *In Love with Norma Loquendi*. New York: Random House, 1994.

————. *What's the Good Word*. New York: Times Books, 1982.

Shachtman, Tom. *The Inarticulate Society: Eloquence and Culture in America*. New York: Free Press, 1995.

Simon, John. *Paradigms Lost: Reflections on Literacy and Its Decline*. New York: Penguin Books, 1981.

Simpson, David. *The Politics of American English, 1776–1850*. New York: Oxford University Press, 1986.

Smitherman, Geneva. *Black Talk: Words and Phrases from the Hood to the Amen Corner*. New York: Houghton Mifflin, 1994.

Stegner, Wallace. *Where the Bluebird Sings to the Lemonade Springs: Living and Writing in the West.* New York: Random House, 1992.

Vidal, Gore. Foreword. In Logan Pearsall Smith, *All Trivia: A Collection of Reflections and Aphorisms.* New York: Ticknor & Fields, 1984.

Werner, Doug, and Steve Badillo. *Skateboarder's Start-Up.* San Diego: Tracks Publishing, 2000.

————. *Skateboarding: New Levels.* Chula Vista, Calif.: Tracks Publishing, 2002.

Whitman, Walt. *Complete Poetry and Collected Prose.* New York: Library of America, 1982.

Wilson, Kenneth G. *Rip Van Winkle's Return: Changes in American English, 1966–1986.* Hanover, N.H.: University Press of New England, 1987.

INDEX

computer databases for, 25, 193
constant change in, 1
dialect diversity in, 31–48, 78, 86–87, 198
ethnic diversity and, 169–70, 199–200
future of, 6–7, 152, 197–201
global role of, 1–4, 44
myths about, 7–8, 18, 35
national vs. local standards of, 53–54
number of speakers of, 3
regional prejudice and, 5, 54–58
Spanish language and, 8, 80, 91, 107–14
standard, 5, 6, 197
supposed homogenizing of, 7, 78
varieties of, 4–5
see also written American English; *specific varieties*
Americanisms:
British adoption of, 2–3
in *OED*, 4, 18–19
recent examples of, 25–26
see also slang
American National Corpus, 25
American Speech, 65
Ammiano, Tom, 172–73, 174
Angelou, Maya, 24
Ann Arbor, Mich., 131–32, 142
Anniston, Ala., 72–74
anti-Semitism, 56
Appalachia, 50, 68–73
Arabic language, 190
Arkansas, 5, 55
Arnott, Kirk, 61–62
Ash, Sharon, 39
Asian Americans, 116, 157, 159–60, 170
Associated Press, 20
Atlantic Monthly, The, 16–17
Atlas of North American English, 36, 37, 67

Australia, 38, 73
axe, ask, 117

Badillo, Steve, 166–67
Bailey, Guy, 36, 81–82, 86, 120–22, 124–26
Bailon, Gilbert, 97–98
Baldwin, James, 129–30, 133–34
Bangalore, 47
"Barely Audible" (Hodge), 136–37
Baron, Dennis, 10, 44, 47, 58, 103–04, 106, 175–76, 200
Bauer, Laurie, 17
Baugh, John, 47–48, 118, 127, 128, 131–33, 140, 184, 186, 198
BBC, 5, 35
be, invariant, 124, 126
Beat Generation, 130, 153
Beavers, Sandy, 171–72
Beverly Hills High School, 156
Blackburn, Linda, 81
Black Talk (Smitherman), 116
Blake, Renée, 140
blame systems, 188
bleedover effect, 68
Bligen, Benjamin, 119–20
bling bling, 147
Blue Music, 20
BMW, 186–90
Bonfiglio, Thomas Paul, 56
Bono, 199–200
Boston, Mass., 31, 33, 49, 85
Brinkley, Douglas, 76
British English, 2–4, 50–53, 57, 73, 154
British Received Pronunciation, 50
brokers, 43
Brooks, David, 105

Federal Communications Commission (FCC), 199

feminism, 170, 175

Florida, 89, 98, 106

folk vocabularies, 36

Fontenot, Blackie, 78–79

Foreign Policy, 104

Fought, Carmen, 48, 110–12, 161, 162–63, 168, 176

Fought, John, 58, 62–63, 66, 71

Fowler, H. G., 9, 23, 60, 61

Fox, Vicente, 102, 112

Fox News Channel, 28

Foxworthy, Jeff, 77, 185

France, 95

Franklin, Benjamin, 49–50, 94

French Academy, 14

French language, 39, 78–80

Fresh Air, 15–16

Friedman, Kinky, 82

Friends, 3

fuck, 171, 199–200

Fuentes, Carlos, 103, 112

Garcia, Robert, 99–100

Gates, Bill, 179

Gauchat, Louis, 41

gender diversity, 170

gender stereotyping, computer speech and, 181, 186–88

generational differences, 74–75, 105, 110, 112, 126, 168, 176

Georgia, 5, 31, 85

German immigrants, 46, 50, 78, 80, 93–95

German language, 60, 93–94

ghetto fab vernacular, 161

Gibson, Calvin, 175

Ginsberg, Allen, 153

girl, 175

girls, teenage, 155–61

see also Valley Girl English

Goff, Jayk, 167–68

Goldberg, Whoopi, 144

Gordon, Matthew, 38–39

Graddol, David, 190

Grammar Hotlines, 60–61

Grandagent, Charles H., 56

grapholect, 60

Great Britain, *see* British English; England

Gullah, 33, 118–20

guy, 175

Haberman, Clyde, 26

Halpern, Mark, 16–17, 141

Hanson, Victor David, 104

Harlem, 115, 128, 130, 136

Harper Dictionary of Contemporary Usage, 63–64

Harvard University, 56

Hayakawa, S. I., 105–06

Heckerling, Amy, 156–57

Hemingway, Ernest, 14

Hicks, Ray and Rosa, 68–69

Hillbilly dialect, 69

Hindi-Urdu language, 190

hip-hop, 4, 20, 141–47

Hip Hop Nation Language, 144

Hispanics, *see* Spanish-speaking immigrants and residents

Historical Dictionary of American Slang, 19

Hodge, Chinaka, 136–37

A Note About the Authors

ROBERT MacNEIL and WILLIAM CRAN are the co-authors of *The Story of English* (with Robert McCrum). The co-anchor of PBS's *The MacNeil/Lehrer NewsHour* until his retirement in 1995, Robert MacNeil is also the author of three volumes of memoirs and three novels, including, most recently, *Breaking News*. He lives in New York City. William Cran has produced many documentary series for British and American television. He lives in London.

A Note about the Type

The text of this book is set in Baskerville MT,
designed by John Baskerville (1706–1775).
This font belongs to the Transitional period in type design,
in which the characters have a linear, austere appearance.
The modern revival of Baskerville's designs began in the 1920s,
and soon afterward all of the major type foundries
had their own versions of Baskerville.